The International Trading System

The World Trade Organization (WTO) is without doubt one of the main instruments of globalization, and the controversy which is whipped up by this organization is arguably mainly caused by the mystery which surrounds it. *The International Trade System* seeks to remove the clouds of misunderstanding that circle the multilateral commercial system by clearly describing and explaining the processes, conventions and rules according to which world trade functions.

The latest developments in the international trade system can be understood with more clarity after reading this book. Academics and students of international economics, finance and business will find this an impressive read.

Alice Landau has been Invited Professor at the University of Montréal and Calgary, Canada. She is Senior Lecturer at the University of Geneva and is a consultant to the US government, the European Commission and several international organizations based in Geneva, Switzerland.

Routledge studies in the Modern World Economy

To Frank Pfetsch

The International Trading System

Alice Landau

Routledge
Taylor & Francis Group

LONDON AND NEW YORK

First published 2005 by Routledge
2 Park Square, Milton Park, Abingdon, Oxon OX14 4RN

Simultaneously published in the USA and Canada
by Routledge
270 Madison Ave, New York, NY 10016

Routledge is an imprint of the Taylor & Francis Group

© 2005 Alice Landau

Typeset in Times by Keystroke, Jacaranda Lodge, Wolverhampton
Printed and bound in Great Britain by TJ International Ltd, Padstow, Cornwall

British Library Cataloguing in Publication Data
A catalogue record for this book is available from the British Library

Library of Congress Cataloging in Publication Data
A catalog record for this book has been requested

ISBN 0–415–32256–1

Contents

Illustrations

Foreword

The process of globalization rolls on with ever-increasing momentum. It presents mankind with some difficult choices: how to handle the energy–environment conundrum, with more and more dependence upon the fossil fuels which result in global warming? How to guarantee safe and fair trade among nations? How to bring about lasting peace?

International relations expert Alice Landau makes an enquiry into the first and most advanced aspect of modernization in her new book: *The International Trading System*. This analysis of all the complexities and ambiguities that characterize the WTO is most welcome, because it is a unique piece of scholarship. Penetrating behind the façade of more than 50 years' struggle over the basic conditions for economic interaction between countries could only be accomplished by a scholar living in Geneva, knowing the WTO inside and out.

When creating and enforcing the WTO system a whole series of games unfolds among the major players in the world economy. On the one hand, common solutions are Pareto-efficient but individual players can always opt for more. When they do so, meetings are deadlocked or simply break down. It takes a long time to reach agreement regarding the key issues at these games, which is why the WTO system has a long history which involves both dramatic breakthroughs as well as stunning failures. Landau shows that the more learning there is and the more future-orientated the individual players become, the more hope we may place on Geneva coordinating trade and commerce. This book is essential reading for students of globalization.

Professor Jan Erik Lane
University of Geneva

Abbreviations

ACP	Africa Caribbean Pacific
AGOA	African Growth and Opportunity Act
ATC	Agreement on Textiles and Clothing
BOP	balance of payments provisions
CACM	Central American Common Market
CAP	Common Agricultural Policy
CCC	Customs Cooperation Council
CEDEAO	Economic and Monetary Union of West Africa
CEMAC	Central African Economic and Monetary Union
CIF	cost, insurance and freight
CJD	Creutzfeldt–Jakob Disease
COMESA	Common Market for South and East Africa
DC	developing country
DSB	Dispute Settlement Body
EC	European Community
ECLA	Economic Commission for Latin America
EFTA	European Free Trade Association
EU	European Union
FAO	Food and Agricultural Organization
GATS	General Agreement on Trade in Services
GATT	General Agreement on Tariffs and Trade
GMO	genetically modified organisms
GSM	global support measure
GSP	Generalized System of Preferences
IMF	International Monetary Fund
IOE	International Office of Epizooties
ISO	International Standards Organization
LDC	least-developed countries
MAI	Multilateral Agreement on Investments
MFA	Multifibre Arrangement

MFN	Most Favoured Nation
NAFTA	North American Free Trade Agreement
NGO	non-governmental organization
NIC	Newly Industrialized Countries
OECD	Organization for Economic Cooperation and Development
OMPI	see WIPO
PMP	processes and methods of production
S&D	special and differential
SACU	South African Customs Union
SADC	South African Development Community
SCM	Subsidies and Compensatory Measure
SGS	System of Generalized Preferences
SPS	Sanitary and Phytosanitary Measures
TBT	Technical Barriers to Trade
TMB	Textile Monitoring Body
TRIMS	Trade-Related Investment Measures
TRIPS	Trade-Related Intellectual Property Rights
UEMOA	West African Economic and Monetary Union
UNCTAD	United Nations Conference on Trade and Development
VERs	voluntary export restrictions
WIPO	World Intellectual Property Organization
WTO	World Trade Organization

Introduction

The World Trade Organization (WTO) has become the organization *par excellence* for dealing with international trade. The transformation of the General Agreement on Tariffs and Trade (GATT) into the WTO was a natural phenomenon that accompanied profound changes in the international economic scene. The WTO is, without doubt, one of the main globalization instruments. It has contributed to this by lowering the barriers to trade and liberalizing an ever-increasing number of economic sectors, including those of services and intellectual property, that belong to the national domain, and by shaping the economic policies of member countries. The WTO Agreements assist the activities of transnational enterprises, the principal players in globalization, and the Uruguay Round confirmed this liberalization. From the Geneva Round in 1947 to that of the Uruguay Round in 1986–1994, the level of tariffs applied to industrial products has fallen from 40 per cent to 3.8 per cent, and the reduced tariffs that have been consolidated have facilitated the establishment of a transnational economy.

By establishing a uniform body of rules formulated in the principal Agreements negotiated with more than 115 countries, the WTO ensures the stability and foreseeable nature of commercial operations. The economic players no longer have to fear such governmental practices as ill-timed increases in customs duties or import restrictions. Rules governing services, standards, subsidies and intellectual property rights enable economic operators to organize their production on a multinational scale and to comply with the more converging regulations (Hart 1999: 33). The Marrakesh Agreements favour the predominantly technological sectors (Lawrence 2000). All transactions are subject to national processing. Exceptions are possible, such as for national security, cultural identity, technological sovereignty or sectorial breakdown – but they must be justified. The Marrakesh Agreements have made provision for safeguards: treatment standards for expropriations, and measures of local content.

Each member state is subject to the same rules, has signed the same universal code that is applicable before the export of goods (inspection procedures), when these reach the frontier (evaluation of customs duties and import licences), and – by adopting harmonized requirements – after the goods have entered the territory of the importing country. Unlike its predecessor, the WTO has become a multilateral organization. There were 115 members when the Marrakesh Agreements were signed and this number has now increased to 149, with many countries, including the former USSR, waiting to join. The Doha Summit in December 2001 confirmed the entry of China into the WTO after years of intense negotiation.

The WTO: an overcast future

The WTO has not won unanimous acceptance, however, and its future remains uncertain. It is the target of anti-globalists, anarchists and anti-free-marketeers. The anti-WTO demonstrations in Seattle in December 1999 served to unite the voices raised against free trade and the growing ascendancy of globalization – against a free trade that has not succeeded in ensuring an equitable distribution of profits. Criticism comes from the unions, environmentalists, consumers and militants for human rights. The WTO Ministerial Meeting served to mobilize these different groups, and constituted a rallying ground similar to that of the annual International Monetary Fund meeting, the Davos forum and the G8 meeting in Genoa. These groups aspire to another way of living and accuse the WTO of trading away human rights, health and the environment for purely commercial reasons. According to these critics, the WTO is penalizing the environment for the sake of easing trade restrictions. It is encouraging transnational enterprises to reduce staff and relocate their activities in 'paradises' where environmental and social standards are less strict. These arguments are certainly justified in the view of those who criticize the WTO, but very few among them have a real knowledge of the aims, purposes and operation of the organization that they are seeking to attack. The present work, devoted to the functioning of the multilateral system of trade, is, therefore, an essential instrument in demystifying this organization.

Guy de Jonquières offers an explanation for the scepticism shown by the public (2000: 26). The end of communism led to a general acceptance of the liberal credo and market economy, but at the same time it removed its main source of legitimacy: American patronage. When communism divided the world, the United States defended the Western democracies against communism. But with the ending of the Cold War, the USA has become reluctant to assume all the burdens involved and to support multi-lateralism.

American trade policy has changed and the coalition for free trade has become fragmented, while the influence of environmentalists and other pressure groups has increased. As enthusiastic defenders of multilateralism, the USA nevertheless appears to question its efficacy by resorting to means that it denounces elsewhere. It favours bilateralism – when it is not practising unilateralism – in the management of world affairs. It is disassociating itself from the very processes that it helped to create. It has a desire for 'managed trade', in which it compels its business partners to open up their markets. The USA is practising a double policy – it ostensibly makes the GATT one of the keystones of its policy while threatening its trade partners more frequently than previously with retaliatory measures, based on Section 301 that threatens countries employing distortive policies.[1] The refusal of Congress to grant the 'fast track' to the President corroborates the weakening of the liberal credo that has always motivated the world's greatest trading power.

Another cloud threatens the WTO. The failure of the ministerial meeting in Seattle that was to initiate the next millennium negotiations has cast doubt in people's minds. Seattle was based on a gamble that could not be sustained: it concerned organizing vast negotiations or none at all. There was no middle way. In order to carry on negotiations it was impossible to be satisfied solely through having recourse to the 'built-in' provisions of the Marrakesh Agreements. Japan and the European Union, supported by several developing countries, were in favour of broader agreements that would include access to markets in the area of agriculture and services, anti-dumping, subsidies, technical obstacles to trade and new challenges such as investments, competition, electronic commerce and biotechnology. They sought to strengthen the multilateral commercial system by integrating rights and obligations in areas that have come to the fore since the Uruguay Round.

According to Pascal Lamy, the EU Trade Commissioner, negotiations concerning competition are indispensable for ensuring development, for under-development means monopoly rents, cartels and opaque and corrupt public procurements (http://www.wto.org). The WTO should not apologize for the unacceptable face of capitalism. The American administration, paying no heed to the opinion of those academics in favour of starting new negotiations, has confined itself to narrow negotiations that only concern provisions in the agreements that would have the advantage of being concluded rapidly. Countries could not agree on the content of the negotiations. A large number of proposals were put forward but the divisions between the delegations were too great. None of them could agree on the draft, the basic document for starting the negotiations. As affirmed by Jacquet, the setback at Seattle was that of American leadership (2001: 408–413).

The WTO and the developing countries: friends of enemies?

The developing countries, which submitted more than two hundred proposals during the preparatory phase of the Seattle Conference, called for numerous changes in the agreements and the inclusion of discussion of their specific problems, such as the operationalization of the special and differentiated treatment that had been accorded to them (Ganesan 2000: 86). Some of them were of the opinion that new negotiations would be impossible before the application of the Uruguay Round Agreements had been completed. They were anxious to obtain an extension of the transition periods that they had obtained during the Uruguay Round in order to enable them to deal with the obligations of the agreements (Das 2000: 187). Aware of the effect of the agreements on their own national systems and institutions, they were only willing to negotiate on such specific subjects as the transparency of public procurements, competition or facilitating trade (Wattal 2000: 77). They considered that negotiating investments was in their interest, but continued to oppose the inclusion of environmental or social standards on the agenda. It was difficult to reconcile these two divergent positions. The WTO found itself caught between the demonstrations by the opponents of globalization, the divergent points of view of the negotiators and the demands of developing countries, individually or in serried ranks within coalitions. Indeed, casting aside the passivity that had characterized the developing countries before the Uruguay Round, these countries now abandoned their reticence towards the GATT and claimed their right to speak.

The change of US opinion enabled a favourable outcome in Doha. The USA was in favour of new negotiations, whose constituent elements were similar to those supported by the members of the European Union. Before the Doha meeting commenced, however, the developing countries made clear their refusal to enter into new negotiations on which the two major trading powers had come to an agreement. In order not to endanger the results of Doha and allow the negotiations to fail, the USA listened to the developing countries and gave them what they had been seeking since the United Nations Conference on Trade and Development (UNCTAD) X in Bangkok, in 1988 – the right to manufacture the generic drugs required in the fight against AIDS, but which bypass the discipline of intellectual property rights. The threat of disputes in the generic domain did not apply to the Sub-Saharan countries. The developing countries also scored another victory. The social rights that the USA had claimed since Seattle did not form part of the Doha package. The USA agreed to downplay their demands for the application of trade sanctions to countries that would not respect social standards. The negotiators recognized the ILO as the reference organ for these. The difficulties encountered by developing countries in applying the agreements were the subject of a separate declaration. After September 11th, it appeared that both developed and developing countries had formed a united front on an economic agenda.

The method of the weak

By following isolationist trade policies since the 1970s, developing countries had remained marginal within the GATT for a long time, but the situation at the close of the 1980s was quite different. They had accepted the path of economic liberalism and this engagement was to change their view of the international system. Their attention was no longer focused exclusively on the structural deficiencies of the international system, but on their mutual trade interests. As stressed by Rubens Ricupero, developing countries need the safety net provided by multilateral rules (http://www.unctad.org). They need this more than other countries, because they are weak. They are no longer seeking to replace the trade system by an alternative based on their own rules. Now there is no other trade system than that practised by the WTO. They subscribe to the multilateral discipline because this is more capable of increasing their negotiating power. Developing countries adhere to a system based on international standards and principles. Developing countries thus increase their credibility and acquire power, despite an inequality at the level of their resources and means. It was this power that they used at Seattle.

The Seattle ministerial conference is an example of the method used by weak countries to overcome their handicap by inspiring stricter rules and moral principles in the negotiations. Throughout the conference the developing countries were excluded from the 'green room' discussions, a caucus of about thirty key players and working parties who met in order to arrive at a consensus in areas of conflict. The USA upset the developing countries by requiring the establishment of rules that would sanction countries that violated basic working rights in order to reduce their production costs. The developing countries won over some of the developed countries to their cause and demanded that their rights be respected and their status be more equal within the organization.

The African countries, that had hitherto been marginalized during the Uruguay Round, then mobilized. Their main preoccupation continued to be the preferences that the EU had granted them. During the Seattle meeting they rose up against American attempts to include social standards in the agenda, arguing that this demand was an attempt at disguised protectionism and would harm their comparative advantage. The Latin American and Caribbean countries joined with the Organization for African Unity (OAU) in threatening to leave the negotiations and reject any agreement negotiated without their approval.

The weak countries once more employed the strategy they had used during the Uruguay Round and inspired moral principles by criticizing the lack of transparency in the WTO and the impact of the negotiations, the sole purpose of which was economic. Developing countries are not without certain advantages. They outnumber the developed countries, comprising more than 100 out of a total of 136 states. In the negotiations, all the players are interdependent and all of them can secure advantages (Kelman 1996: 99). Advantages create dependence. Each actor is dependent in order to secure the assigned objectives in the negotiations (Habeeb 1988: 18)

In 1999, UNCTAD asked whether it was in the interest of developing countries to negotiate with the rich countries. Their chronic weakness in terms of research, intellectual and analytical support, and their negotiation power, put them in an inferior position. Many developing countries do not have permanent missions in Geneva. At the moment there are sixty-five missions from developing countries in Geneva, twenty-six countries continue to be represented by missions in Paris, Berlin or Brussels. Some of these countries consider their relations with the EU to be more important than those with the WTO. The missions are also depleted. They only have two or three diplomats, as against the developed countries with four to six (*The Observer*, 5 December 1999).

All the developed countries and the majority of those in transition are represented in Geneva; certain of these have two missions, one of which specializes in the WTO. Some developing countries, such as Uganda, Zambia and Zimbabwe, have moved to Geneva. Their lack of participation is visible in many of the committees created subsequent to the Marrakesh Agreements. Developing countries prefer to remain silent in order to hide their ignorance (Lal Das 1999: 160).

Broad negotiations have many advantages and enable the negotiators to obtain concessions and achieve the aims that they have set themselves. Economic agreements are rarely the outcome of a single negotiation, but consist of several parallel negotiations conducted separately by different people. These multiple negotiations give rise to constructive attitudes for solving problems and for trade-offs between the issues. An agenda that comprises several sections in which the issues are discussed together maximizes the number of possible combinations and compromises. As Homans has stressed: 'the greater the number of issues that can be divided into values appreciated by the negotiators, the greater the chances of success' (in Landau 2000: 19). The parties present are then able to negotiate different issues to their mutual advantage. As Jönsson humorously expressed it: 'instead of juggling with one ball at the time, the negotiators throw all the balls in the air in order to find the ideal combination' (in Zartman 1986: 278–301).

According to Fred Bergsten (1998), initiating new negotiations is essential to further the liberalization bi-round. Every halt in trade negotiations gives rise to new protectionist barriers. As a privileged instrument to resolve the trade disputes that never cease to grow under the influence of economic interdependence, a new round is essential to maintain multilateralism. The post-Kennedy Round was marked by a revival of protectionist practices in the United States, which adopted the Mills Law, imposing quotas on textile products and footwear, and set up a harsh control of imports and direct investments. The Nixon administration concluded the Multifibre Arrangement (MFA) and introduced the 'Super 301' Law that was designed to take retaliatory measures against countries that did not go along with the rules for the conduct of trade as stated by the United States. These protectionist initiatives can be explained by the absence of any GATT negotiation (Bergsten 1998). Certain observers are eager to conclude that if the WTO does not start short-term trade negotiations, countries will turn towards regionalism in order to increase liberalization, with the risk of creating conflicts with the multilateral trade system.

Several groups have been working away at this task and about 60 per cent of world trade has been liberalized by regional efforts. The EU is a striking example. The conclusion of the single market has liberalized the movement of goods, capital, services and people within the community territory. Certain observers stress that the United States appears to be more preoccupied with the NAFTA (North American Free Trade Agreement) and the APEC (Asia-Pacific Economic Cooperation) than with WTO negotiations.

Asian countries would sever connections with the international system in order to reduce their vulnerability, rather than continuing to use exports as a development motor. Already in 1992, the United States was using NAFTA to influence the GATT agenda. It then indicated to its other trading partners that, in the absence of any agreement, it would fall back on a regional strategy. The regional agreement completed measures that are not covered, or covered badly, by the GATT. Services, investments and the environment were incorporated in the NAFTA, without having been treated by the GATT. This strategy was both a signal that the United States was sending to the GATT, as well as the manifestation of a desire to impose its vision on the world.

This book sets out to demystify the multilateral commercial system. Its aim is not to give a comprehensive account of all the WTO agreements, but to present the main characteristics of the most important of them – those that have the greatest effect upon the global economic players.

1 The WTO

From disappointment to hope

The International Trade Organization (ITO) had been conceived as a third pillar of the Bretton Woods Agreement, alongside the International Monetary Fund (IMF) and the World Bank. According to the United States and Great Britain, the two great powers who shaped the world after the Second World War, the principles of multilateralism had to apply to the trade system. They reaffirmed the ties between trade policy and international cooperation on many occasions during the 1942 lending agreements, the 1944 Bretton Woods Conference and the San Francisco Conference, which launched the United Nations. The 1945 American proposals stressed that a trade system must be both multinational and non-discriminatory (Goldstein 1993). Great Britain only partially agreed with to the American arguments. Its preferences were more in the direction of a system that not only took account of tariffs and quotas, but also envisaged full employment. Quantitative restrictions remained at the centre of the American system and the two governments were determined to ban them. In 1945, the United States published some proposals for expanding world trade and employment and circulated them widely. They invited fifteen countries to negotiate the reduction of tariffs and other trade barriers. Fourteen countries, with the notable exception of the Soviet Union, accepted the invitation. An International Trade Organization (ITO) thus was created.

The WTO: new features of the world economy

The United States associated quotas with the economic nationalism that had prevailed in the Havana Charter, concluded in March 1948, which was not only to reduce trade barriers but also to envisage agreements on raw materials and full employment policies. But such an ambition was contrary to the more reductionist visions of the American Congress, under the control of the Republicans, who rejected the ITO largely because the United States had not obtained agreement from Great Britain that it would dismantle its trade preferences.

The President of the United States requested an extension of his nego-tiating mandate in 1949 and decided not to submit ratification to the vote by Congress. The next year saw the outbreak of the Korean War and interest in international cooperation was no longer unanimous (Ostry 2000: 52–76). Opposition spread and support for multilateralism weakened. The Havana Charter was not ratified and it became a temporary agreement whose purpose was to regulate international trade (Destler 1995: 34). The GATT covered about one thousand individual tariff concessions, but, moving beyond this context, it was going to adapt to changes in the world economy, i.e. the cre-ation of the European (Economic) Community (E[E]C) in 1957 and the escalation of trade wars between the United States and the EC from the 1970s onwards. The Kennedy Round annexed Part IV regarding developing coun-tries in the GATT. The Tokyo Round introduced nine multilateral codes, such as those relative to technical barriers to trade, public procurements, the interpretation and application of Articles VI, XVI and XXIII (subsidies and anti-dumping) and import licence procedures. But agriculture and textiles continued not to be subject to GATT discipline.

The United States obtained an exemption for agriculture in 1955 and 1972, the Multifibre Arrangement (MFA) was negotiated under the auspices of GATT. The contracting parties attempted to retain certain flexibility in GATT legalism, at least during the first years of its existence. When devel-opment problems became pressing, the GATT adopted the entitlement clause on special and differentiated treatment that enabled developing countries to enjoy exemptions from the GATT agreements (Kennes 1995).

The WTO inherited this past, but it presented very different character-istics. All WTO agreements had to be endorsed by the member states. They represented a *single undertaking*, and all the agreements integrated in the Marrakesh Agreements applied to the 133 members, except for the two multilateral agreements on government purchases and civil aircraft.[1] They differed from the preceding Tokyo Round, in which many agreements were multilateral. Countries could choose whether to belong or not. The mechanism for settling differences represented one of the most original changes in the present trading system. Within the Tokyo Round, each agree-ment was independent and instituted its own system for settling disputes, *The Memorandum of Agreement on the Rules and Procedures Governing the Dispute of Settlements* applied to all WTO agreements on goods, services and intellectual property. There was no longer more than one mechanism for all WTO agreements.

This mechanism is multilateral and was intended as a response to the unilateralist 'drift' at the end of the 1980s. Henceforth, the most powerful countries who tended to have recourse to unilateral retaliatory measures to settle their bilateral trade differences were constrained to use the WTO system for this contingency. For their part, the developing countries no longer hesitated to employ this mechanism to settle their disagreements with the most powerful countries and between themselves. Numerous legal texts were revised by the Marrakesh Agreements in order to improve their application. Measures for anti-dumping, subsidies and evaluation of merchandise for customs duties were adjusted in accordance with current practices and made more transparent in order to enable the rules to enhance trade.

The Marrakesh Agreements not only cover goods. They incorporate new areas of activity, such as services and intellectual property rights, and subject others to multilateral discipline. All the WTO members have concession lists in the services sector. Many developing countries that were reluctant about negotiating services during the opening of the Uruguay Round have made concessions in order to attract investment and rationalize their policy with regard to services. The Marrakesh Agreements protect intellectual property rights and grant developing countries transition periods for adapting their legislation.

Before the Uruguay Round, agriculture was excluded from the considerable tariff reductions that had taken place during the previous negotiation rounds. Certain GATT Articles, moreover, permitted the use of derogations in agriculture. Certain countries were past masters in the art of protecting their agricultural market and in obtaining derogations. At the end of the Uruguay Round, agriculture complied with WTO discipline. Non-tariff measures such as quotas or variable taxes were converted into tariffs and were reduced. The new tariffs were consolidated, and although they are still high, they can be progressively reduced.

The GATT is built on several principles:

* The Most Favoured Nation (MFN) clause, which ensures non-discriminatory treatment. This principle, according to which

   all advantages, favours, privileges or immunities granted by one contracting party to a product originating from or destined for any other country shall, immediately and unconditionally, be extended for the same treatment to any similar product originating or destined for the territory of all other contracting parties

   promotes the cause of liberalization. This principle reduced the transaction costs of the negotiations for the members. All countries having an interest in a product and seeking to improve access to it in an exporting country and having negotiated this concession, must accord the same to every other country.

- The second principle of this system is that of national treatment and is intended to complement the MFN clause. It stipulates that every imported product after payment of the customs duties must not receive less favourable treatment than a local product. Each member state is obliged to treat local and imported products in the same way.
- The third principle is that of transparency. The Marrakesh Agreements reinforce transparency by adjusting notification and information procedures. All laws and regulations must be published, in order to enable other members to consult them and ensure that they conform to the prevailing legal texts in force. Transparency is also the aim of the review mechanism of trade policies. This enables WTO members to examine the implementation of the trade policy of a member state or group of countries within a regional agreement. It gives more transparency to trade policies. At present, the trade policies of the four biggest exporters – the United States, the European Union, Japan and Canada – are examined every two years, those of the sixteen other largest exporters every four years, and those of developing countries every six years. The less advanced countries are not subject to an examination at any fixed period. Many of the developing countries display their very marked interest in a system that enables them to have a better knowledge of the trade policies of other members, to point out defects in the system and to introduce improvements.

Emergence of new trade barriers

Since the Kennedy Round and the Tokyo Round, negotiations have been extended to non-tariff barriers (Table 1.1). But new forms of protectionism are replacing the tariffs that were been reduced during the preceding rounds

Table 1.1 GATT negotiation rounds

Round	Date	Member countries	Trade value (US$)	Average tariff rate (%)
Geneva	1947	23	10 million	35
Annecy	1949	33	—	35
Torquay	1950	34	—	35
Geneva	1952	22	2.5 million	35
Dillon	1960–61	45	4.9 million	35
Kennedy	1962–67	47	40 billion	35
Tokyo	1970–83	118	155 billion	34
Uruguay	1986–94	120+	3.7 trillion	38

Source: WTO reports, various issues, Jackson (2000).

of the Uruguay Round. Governments are continually inventing new barriers in order to limit imports. In 1973, the GATT listed almost 800 non-tariff barriers. Certain studies show that the tariff equivalent of a non-tariff barrier is about 9 per cent (Jackson 2000: 155). These barriers take the form of administrative barriers or 'grey zones' that exist beyond the GATT discipline and may appear in various guises, including the variable tax applied by the EU within the terms of the Common Agricultural Policy (CAP) or the 'voluntary export restrictions' (VERs). In the latter case, countries whose exports are increasing are asked to keep their exports within the limits negotiated with the importers. These arrangements are supposed to be voluntary, but in reality they are less so.

The restrictions are applied to imports from certain countries and are therefore incompatible with GATT rules, which stipulate non-discrimination of imports, and with Article XI of the GATT, which stipulates that there shall be

> no prohibition or restrictions other than customs duties, tariffs and other charges, whether it be through quotas, import or export licences or other measures, shall be introduced by a contracting party on the exports or sales for export of products destined for the territory of another contracting party.
>
> (Jackson 2000)

Certain non-tariff barriers display considerable ingenuity, including the measure introduced by France prescribing that all VCR (video cassette recorder) imports must pass through Poitiers for treatment, or the measure insisting that tinned foods shall be labelled solely in the language of the importing country.

These barriers affect certain agricultural products, textiles, footwear, steel and electrical machines and equipment from Japan and Korea, among others (UNCTAD 1994: 55–57). In the 1990s, these arrangements affected 15 per cent of world trade. More than 33 per cent of the Japanese exports to the EU and the United States were hit by the VERs (Ruigrok *et al*. 1995: 229), which were added to the customs duties, restrictions and compensatory measures. Table 1.2 shows some of the instruments used by developed countries to limit imports. The anti-dumping measures have replaced other instruments previously used. VERs have become the most important instrument of trade policy. However, the EU largely eliminated the use of VERs other than textiles and clothing restraints, anticipating the WTO agreement by three years (Auboin and Laird 1997: 8).

The liberalization process goes beyond the elimination of tariffs and quantitative restrictions of goods, in order to concentrate on political measures

Table 1.2 Measures employed to protect imports, 1979–1988

Countries	Safeguards	Anti-dumping	Compensatory rights	Others	Total
USA	2	427	371	78	878
EU	6	406	13	33	458
Australia	22	478	1	—	458
Canada	1	447	22	—	470

Source: Messerlin (1990).

affecting access to the markets such as standards and regulations, subsidies, the protection of intellectual property, and limitations on the movements of people.

Trade barriers often come in the shape of national regulations, which was the case for the new subjects covered by the WTO: technical obstacles to trade, sanitary and phytosanitary measures, and services. In services, the majority of the trade barriers are in the form of national regulations that, unlike the barriers that affect the trade in goods, do not take on the shape of transparent obstacles imposed by the customs. They appear in various ways: they may limit the number of companies, the number of employees, the number of distribution points, the services that may be offered, the marketing practices and the distribution networks (Feketekuty 2000).

Governments protect their service suppliers by concentrating on local consumption of services (ibid.: 1–3). The weakest provisions on services concern national regulations, although they do have an undoubted influence on the international trade in services. It is difficult to develop a multilateral discipline in an area that is so linked to national sovereignty.

The Uruguay Round negotiations

The negotiations in the Uruguay Round had very strong connections to the Kennedy and Tokyo Rounds. They continued the trade negotiations started in these earlier rounds concerning public procurements, anti-dumping measures, counterfeits and customs evaluation. The agenda of the Uruguay Round, however, was also very different from the previous negotiations as it treated new subjects such as services, intellectual property rights and investments. The Uruguay Round was innovative in promoting transparency and liberalization in the areas that had remained outside multilateral discipline. The trade regime that emerged from the Uruguay Round comprised the legislative corpus of the GATT and twelve annexed agreements, the agreement on services and that on the trade aspects of intellectual property (Table 1.3).

Table 1.3 Principal instruments negotiated in the Uruguay Round

---

A. The Marrakesh Agreement establishing the World Trade Association
B. Multilateral agreements
1. Goods trade (GATT 1994)

Associated agreements
Agreement on the application of Article VI GATT 1994 (customs evaluation)
Agreement on inspection before delivery
Agreement on technical barriers to trade
Agreement on textiles and Clothing (ATC)
Agreement on sanitary and phytosanitary measures
Agreement on import licences
Agreement on safeguards
Agreement on subsidies and compensatory measures
Agreement on the application of Article VI of the GATT 1994 (Anti-dumping)
Agreement on trade-related investment measures (TRIM)
Agreement on textiles and clothes
Agreement on agriculture
Agreement on rules of origin
Agreement on services trade
Agreement on intellectual property rights
Memoranda of agreement and decisions
Memoranda of agreement on the balance of payments of GATT 1994
Memoranda of agreement on the rules for the dispute settlements
Memoranda of agreement on the interpretation of Article II: 1(b) of the GATT
    1994 (consolidation of the tariff concessions
Decision on trade and environment

Negotiations on the accession of the thirty countries wanting to join the WTO were difficult. The countries had to accept a whole series of measures and laws that are contained in the WTO. They sometimes must follow the wishes of the developed countries. Cambodia agreed to stop importing generic drugs after 2007, even though existing poor countries have until 2016 to start honouring drug patents. Rich members also forced it to adopt a maximum agricultural tariff of 60 per cent, even though the United States sometimes charges as much as 121 per cent, and the European union a formidable 252 per cent. Similarly, Cambodia promised never to subsidise agriculture (*The Economist*, 13 September 2003).

Developing countries had to open bilateral negotiations with countries interested in accession, in order to exchange concessions and commit themselves on access to goods and services markets. China had to open its telecommunications and fund management sectors and stop counterfeits. The WTO was better equipped to regulate international trade thanks to the mechanism for settling disputes. It called upon the member states to respect trade rules by correcting deviant behaviour. Settling conflicts was

Table 1.4 Problems treated by the mechanism for settling disputes, 2001

	Complaints notified to the WTO	*Cases under consideration*	*Reports adopted by the Appeal Body and panels*	*Cases settled or inactive*
Period/date	Since 1 January 1995		Since 1 January 1995	Since 1 January 1995
Number	234	16	51	39

Source: www.wto.org/dispute settlement

ensured by consultation procedures, good offices, conciliation and mediation, arbitration, adjudication, and by an appeal structure (Qureshi 1996: 100). Table 1.4 summarizes the problems treated by the mechanism for settling disputes.

The WTO takes as its basis some generally applicable rules and some that prevent deviant practices by states. The first rule consists of ensuring that frontier protection materializes through low tariffs. Quantitative restrictions are forbidden, with the sole exception of problems concerning the balance of payments. Even in this case, the GATT 1994 balance of payments provisions (BOP) forced the member states not to use quantitative restrictions but to give preference to transparent and measurable procedures based on price. The second rule consists of eliminating tariffs and other barriers by means of multilateral negotiations. The reduced tariffs are consolidated and entered in the national lists. More than 98 per cent of imported industrial goods in the developed countries and transition economies were consolidated, and about 73 per cent in the developing countries (DCs).

The Agreement on Sanitary and Phytosanitary Measures and that on Technical Barriers to Trade have been integrated into the rules that are generally applicable (see Table 1.5). It is to these agreements that we shall now turn in Chapters 2 and 3.

Table 1.5 Revision plan of the Marrakesh Agreements

Year	*Measure*
1998	Sanitary and phytosanitary measures (SPM): revision of the operations and application
	Technical barriers to trade (TBT): revision of operations and application
	Trade-related (TRIPS): negotiations aimed at enlarging and improving the agreement on a reciprocal basis

continued

Table 1.5 continued

Year	Measure
1998	Dispute settlements and memoranda of agreement: revision of application
1999	Public procurements: possible extension of cover on a reciprocal basis
	Trade-related investment measures (TRIMS) investment measures: revision of the operations and discussion concerning the provisions of investment and competition policy that could be included in the agreement
2000	Negotiations on agriculture: continuation of the process of reducing export supports and subsidies
	Services: new round of negotiations to achieve greater liberalization
	Revision of trade policies
2001	Revision of the application of the agreement on textiles and clothing
2002	Application of the agreement on textiles and clothing

Source: WTO reports various issues.

2 The Agreement on Sanitary and Phytosanitary Measures

The Agreement on Sanitary and Phytosanitary Measures was negotiated within the shadow of the Agreement on Agriculture. But it was not a new topic on the trade agenda as the League of Nations had been interested in the relations between science and embargos. During the Uruguay Round, when the tariffication of non-tariff barriers was negotiated, attention concentrated on health protection measures that the member states adopted, which were in fact protectionist barriers. Countries had particularly wanted to negotiate these measures since historically, Article XX: B of the GATT, which authorized countries to take the necessary measures to protect the health and life of persons and animals or for the protection of plant life, was vague and needed clarification. The contracting parties could have recourse to the existing multilateral agreement on technical obstructions to trade negotiated during the Tokyo Round, in order to cover certain of their preoccupations about health. But this agreement had a very wide field of application.

In the 1980s, an increasing number of countries had recourse to sanitary and phytosanitary measures in order to protect their local production, and from this arose the necessity for an agreement that would establish a legal framework and introduce more discipline and obligations in this area.

From certain points of view, the SPS (Sanitary and Phytosanitary Measures) Agreement was more constraining than the TBT (Technical Barriers to Trade) Agreement. According to the latter, members might adopt technical regulations and standards when they were necessary to attain legitimate objectives. But the agreement remained imprecise about these very aims that allowed considerable freedom of action on the part of members. On the other hand, the SPS Agreement authorized countries to apply their own measures on a discriminatory basis in case of risk from diseases transmitted by imported products. It authorized them, moreover, provisionally to limit imports as a precautionary measure, in case of an imminent risk of diseases, without the countries necessarily possessing all the scientific proofs. The TBT Agreement contained no provision of this kind.

A difficult equilibrium to establish

The sanitary and phytosanitary measures were intended to protect the lives of people and animals from the risks of additives, contaminants, toxins or other pathogenic organisms. They contained measures intended to avoid any infection arising from foodstuffs, plants or animals (including fish, wild fauna and flora), and from all diseases, organisms and parasites from forests.[1] The agreement did not include measures for the protection of the environment and consumer interests, dealing with the health and well-being of animals other than those treated under the TBT Agreement. The agreement covered all the laws, regulations and decrees concerning criteria relative to the products, processes and methods of production, testing and inspection procedures, quarantine systems, sampling and risk evaluation methods, packaging, and labelling relative to the harmlessness of the foodstuffs. Processes and methods of production are assuming ever greater importance. They are central to a certain number of actions taken by the EU, especially in matters concerning hormones and fish imports from East Africa. The case of the European Community measures concerning meat and hormones is equally illustrative.[2]

The agreement must fulfil two requirements that have been formulated by the Secretariat:

> How to ensure that consumers of one's country obtain healthy food according to the standards considered to be appropriate, and at the same time how to ensure that health regulations and those relative to health are not utilised for protecting local producers.
>
> (Pardo Quintillãn 1999: 153)

Measures adopted by a country may materialize as trade restrictions. The agreement forbids any unjustified measure equivalent to protection. The agreement is based on scientific tests and recognizes the possibility of countries establishing their own level of sanitary and phytosanitary protection. Article 5 defines this as the level of protection that the member state considers necessary to protect human beings, animals, plants, and health within its territory. The agreement also encourages member states to harmonize their sanitary measures on the basis of standards, orientation and recommendations adopted at an international level.

A country may impose a level of health protection that is higher than would be possible under the WTO agreement and stricter than would be adopted at an international level, on the condition that it is *scientifically justified* (Article 3.3). The state must carry out an evaluation of the risks, as defined by agreement, on the adverse effects on human and animal health arising from the presence of additives, contaminants, toxins or organisms in the food or drink. Article 5 stipulates that the evaluation must take account of the evaluation techniques developed by the international organizations. When the scientific evidence is insufficient, a member state may nevertheless adopt a provisional measure based on the available information and for a reasonable period of time, and thus apply a precautionary principle. Article 5, paragraph 7, stipulates that, in the case where the scientific proofs are insufficient, a member state may provisionally adopt sanitary standards based on pertinent information that is available, including that which comes from international organizations.

The agreement clearly establishes the parameters of action for states in the sanitary domain and recommends scientific proof, harmonization, equivalence and mutual recognition, risk evaluation and transparency. International standards are able to prevent trade distortions. The aim of the agreement is to find a balance between the levels of health protection introduced by the member states, while preventing the adopted measures from becoming a disguised form of protectionism.

The fundamental question raised by the agreement concerns the role of science and the treatment of the cases where there is scientific uncertainty. The SPM Agreement authorizes immediate and unilateral action in an emergency situation, even where the proof is insufficient. According to William Davey, the cases that arise from the Agreement on Sanitary and Phytosanitary Measures submitted for the settlement of disputes are among the most controversial. Risk evaluation gives rise to considerable litigation. There has to be a reasonable connection between the measure and the risk evaluation. Thus, in the case of hormone-treated beef, the measure adopted by the EU, as well as that of Australia in the case of salmon, was not based on the evaluation of risks (Davey 2001: 90).

The agreement applies to genetically modified organisms (GMO). These, at least in the EU countries, are the object of strict regulations concerning the risks involved, authorization of sale, control and labelling. The absence of harmonized rules leads necessarily to trade distortions and preoccupations concerning their potential effect on health and the environment. The EU regulatory programme rests on an evaluation of the risks carried out in member states at community level and labelling in order to keep the consumer informed about the GMO content in the product, which are obligatory if this measure is scientifically justified. Nevertheless, as Pardo Quintillän (1999) has noted, labelling proves difficult, because all the harvests are mixed together when they arrive in Europe, and there is no way of separating genetically modified products from those that are not.

The mixture is also unavoidable because the packaging is done in bulk and no special treatment was envisaged for GMO products (Davey 2001:

182). Since 1998, the EU has frozen all authorization for the sale of these goods in the EU territory. The EU finds itself in a dilemma, however, between the desire to respect the consumer who manifests opposition to consuming GMO and the desire to avoid inflaming the already difficult relations with the United States. A definitive embargo on GMO would be a measure to reassure the consumer about the risks involved, but politically it would be a difficult one to take.

Obligations of the SPS Agreement

At the level of rights and obligations, the agreement adopts the fundamental principles of the GATT. The sanitary and phytosanitary measures must not be discriminatory. The SPS Agreement requires transparency. Transparency, as in many of the agreements, is essential, especially for those concerned with technical obstacles to trade. Transparency guarantees that the SPS measures are used for the protection of health and avoid, as far as possible, being protectionist. All measures must be notified, well before their adoption. The exporting countries concerned by these measures may offer their comments on the regulation projects within a period of thirty days.

The SPS Agreement recommends the adoption of international standards, directives and international recommendations (Codex Alimentarius, Directives of the International Office in Paris for the Epizootic Diseases of Animals, and the International Convention for the Protection of Plants in Rome). The SPS Agreement recognizes these three organizations that have set up scientific standards in the areas of human and animal health and the protection of plant life.

The SPS Agreement identifies the competent organizations for developing and adopting international standards more clearly than the TBT Agreement, but leaves the door open for other organizations that could legislate concerning them, such as the International Convention for the Protection of Plant Life, set up at the Food and Agricultural Organization (FAO) for the protection of plant life, introduced at the FAO (CIPV), the mixed FAO/WHO Commission of the Codex Alimentarius (Codex) and the International Office of Epizooties (IOE).[3] Developing countries should participate actively in the standardization activities, and in training programmes at international and national levels.[4] Developed countries must distribute the information they possess concerning regulations, standards and certification requirements among exporters.

The agreement compels members to adopt equivalent measures. Exporters must show that the measures they adopt reach the same level of protection as those of the importing country. They must submit tests so that the latter can analyse them. The importer may send inspectors on site to check the standards employed. The Codex has developed standards destined to define the equivalence of these measures.

Box 1.1 The case of mad cow disease

States take account of economic factors when they protect the health of human beings, plants and animals. The case of mad cow disease is a case in point. The authorities had waited a long time before adopting measures, because the costs, from the financial and political point of view, of eradicating the disease were enormous. In 1996, public and scientific opinion was preoccupied with the effect of mad cow disease (Creutzfeldt–Jakob Disease (CJD)) and its responsibility for the death of several people. Concerned by the relationship between CJD and a new form of the disease, the EU imposed an embargo on the import of beef from the United Kingdom.

The embargo was provisional and had to continue until scientific proofs were established. After these had proved the existence of a relation between the consumption of beef and a new form of the Creutzfeldt–Jakob Disease, the embargo was maintained. Criticisms were raised. The arguments of the detractors concentrated on the source of the proofs. In this case, the EU took precautionary measures against the possible risks to human health. These were challenged by the UK. The European Court of Justice decided that in a case of doubt concerning a health risk, the proof should reside in the possibility of a risk. This proof justified the embargo, which was finally lifted in 1998.

Special provisions for developing countries

Developing countries may benefit from technical assistance, either bilaterally or through the intermediary of international bodies, on behalf of the Codex, the IOE, the CIPV and the WHO, in the areas of processing techniques, research and infrastructure.

They also have special and differentiated treatment at their disposal in the development of regulations, standards and sanitary and phytosanitary prescriptions (Article 10). Article 10 indicates that in the development and application of SPS measures, members should take account of the special needs of developing countries, and, in the implementation of new SPS measures, developing countries should have longer time limits to comply with them.

Developing countries have limited and specific exceptions from the obligations arising from the agreement. Their participation in the international organizations should be assisted and encouraged. Certain developing countries have noted that these provisions are not applied in a satisfactory way and make more precise proposals within the WTO and other standardizing organizations recognized by the agreement, concerning – among other things – transition periods.

Developing countries may profit from an agreement that sets out uniform rules, irrespective of their political weight, economic power or technological means. Without such an agreement, developing countries would be more exposed to the will of importing countries.

The SPS Committee is entrusted with managing the SPS Agreement. The Committee constitutes a forum of negotiation and communication for the member states. All members have the opportunity to inform the Committee of all the regulations and standards adopted by other Members that would interfere with their exports. Notifications need to be more widely used in order for countries to be better informed on the regulations, and to enable developing countries to be better able to challenge those who prohibit their exports.

Up to the present, developing countries have not been able to fully employ all the provisions of the agreement, as well as all the means of appeal that are offered to them, especially by the Committee. Concerning challenging adopted measures, there is a lack of coordination at administrative levels and between these and the exporters. Developing countries that often face similar problems and have the same interests to defend should adopt a strategic alliance to form a united front.

Having disussed the main provisions of the Agreement of Sanitary and Phytosanitary Measures, we shall now turn to the Agreement on Technical Barriers to Trade in Chapter 3.

3 The Agreement on Technical Barriers to Trade

Since the creation of the GATT, tariffs have decreased and have been consolidated. During the Uruguay Round, consolidations increased from 78 to 99 per cent for developed countries, 21 to 73 per cent for developing countries and 73 to 98 per cent for economies in transition. All non-quantitative import restrictions have been tariffed, thus enabling the introduction of greater transparency in the agricultural domain and making way for the lowering of tariffs in this area of activity.

Since the 1970s, however, the contracting parties have shown their concern at being confronted by the appearance of non-tariff barriers, and have come to the conclusion that technical barriers form the greatest deterrent to trade. The expression 'technical barriers' applies to the standards, but may equally comprise quotas and import licences. In view of the increase in problems applied to inspections, the Tokyo Round negotiated a code for standards, the aim of which was to adopt and apply regulations, standards and procedures to evaluate conformity.

The Agreement on the Technical Barriers to Trade (TBT) was based on the Tokyo Round's code and reinforced its obligations. The purpose of the agreement was to ensure that the regulations WTO members adopt do not create unnecessary barriers to international trade. The text of the agreement states that:

> Members shall act in such a way that the technical regulations are not prepared, adopted or applied with a view to or with the effect of creating unecessary obstacles to international trade.[1] For this purpose, technical regulations shall not be more trade-restrictive than necessary to fulfil a legitimate objective taking account of the risks non-fulfilment would create.

The agreement specifies the legitimate objectives thus: 'These legitimate objectives are, among others, national security requirements, the prevention of deceptive practices, protection of the health or safety, animal or plant life or health, or the environment'. The TBT Agreement covers all industrial and agricultural products except those included in the sanitary and phytosanitary measures, their characteristics, the processes and methods of production (PMP) that affect the characteristics of the product, the terminology, symbols and regulations concerning the packaging and labelling that apply to a product. The obligations of the agreement exceed the requirements for non-discrimination and raise the question of the necessary scientific justifications for adopting standards that affect imports. The agreement makes reference to international standards. According to John Jackson, the TBT and SPM Agreements, although similar, differ fundamentally on the means employed for detecting whether a measure is of a protectionist nature. The TBT Agreement is based on tests for detecting whether a measure discriminates against an imported product. As for the SPM Agreement, it concentrates on scientific principles and risk evaluation tests (Jackson 2000: 224).

Regulations, standards and evaluation procedures for conformity

The agreement recognizes that non-governmental groups may enact standards and that producers may approach bodies entrusted with the adoption of standards during their drafting. The text recommends transparency and encourages the parties to recognize the tests. But it stresses that the procedures for evaluating conformity shall not have the intention or the effect of creating unnecessary barriers to international trade. This means, among other things, that the procedures for the evaluation of conformity will not be more strict or applied in a way that is stricter than necessary to give an importing member sufficient reassurance that the products are in conformity with the technical regulations or applicable standards, having regard to the risks that non-conformity would entail.

The TBT Agreement and the international organizations

The agreement applies the fundamental principles of the GATT – the most favoured nation and national treatment clauses – and specifies that non-discrimination shall apply to the different stages in the preparation, adoption and application of the technical regulations and standards.

The agreement encourages members to adopt technical regulations and standards that are based on the performances of the products rather than on their conceptual properties. The agreement recommends the use of technical regulations and international standards, which substitute effectively for the multitude of regulations and standards adopted by member states, except where the government considers that they would be ineffective or ill-adapted to their climatic, geographic or technical conditions. Such an exception is also possible when the technology necessary for the application of an international standard is not available in the country concerned.

Members are invited to participate actively, within the limits of their resources, in the work of the International Standards Organization (ISO) and the many other institutions (about fifty) concerned with international standardization, such as the International Electrotechnical Commission, the International Telecommunications Union, the International Tropical Timber Association, the World Health Organization (WHO), and the Codex Alimentarius of the FAO/WHO for food products, in order to draft international standards.

Equivalence and mutual recognition: the pillars of the agreement

The WTO recommends its members be a party to these negotiations with a view to a mutual recognition of the regulations. These mutually recognized agreements extend to the evaluation procedures. The aim is to avoid increasing the evaluation procedures (in the exporting and importing countries) and financial costs. Mutual recognition is of major importance, especially for developing countries. These can set up national standardization bodies, which facilitate on-the-spot inspections, and in doing so rely on the international bodies, such as the ISO and other institutions.

One of the aims of the single market within the EU has been to harmonize regulations and technical standards through the principle of mutual recognition (judgment on the Cassis of Dijon by the European Court of Justice in 1978). But harmonization is far from being applied. The lack of standardization between member states is particularly marked in the areas of consumer and environmental protection.

The transparency principle is a central feature of the TBT Agreement, and is applied by the notification of technical regulations and standards before they come into force, particularly when they do not conform to international rules. Obligatory regulations have to be notified to the WTO, and standards to the ISO centre via the ISONET data path. Notifications do not necessarily ensure conformity of a regulation with the WTO Agreement. A notified regulation may be challenged by one or several members because it does not conform in substance or application to the agreement. They have a time limit of thirty days in which to do this. The problem often resides in the long delays in circulating a regulation among the competent bodies in the developing countries.

Each member is also under obligation to set up one or several information points qualified to answer all questions concerning regulations, standards and conformity procedures. This requirement is different from the requirement to notify technical regulations. Notifications and information points must contribute to settling the information problem, which is particularly sensitive in developing countries.

The agreement established a committee for the technical barriers to trade, an actual negotiating framework for the members. The TBT Committee, which meets three times a year, is responsible for managing the agreement. The Committee constitutes a negotiation and discussion forum for the member states. Every member is permitted to alert the Committee about all regulations and standards adopted by other members that might harm their exports. The country concerned must justify itself. The committee does not necessarily discuss all the notifications that are presented to it, but it does so whenever several members contest the conformity of a regulation.

Up to the present, developing countries have not been in a position to use the committee. They have been unable, as requested by the developed countries, to draw up a list of concrete cases where they were unable to conform to the technical regulations.

Special provisions for developing countries

According to Article 11 of the agreement, developed countries are under obligation to provide, upon request, technical assistance to developing countries to help them to develop technical regulations for compliance with the technical regulations in force in the export markets, to participate in the work of the international bodies and to support them. Priority is given to the less advanced countries. These are exempted from the principal obligations of the agreement. Developed countries must avoid having recourse to international standards if developing countries cannot utilize them in their own countries.

Several developing and developed countries have recently expressed the desire to identify international standardization organizations by way of the TBT Agreement and have reserved the right to judge the appropriateness of the international standards. Developing countries are frequently under the impression that the standards developed at international level do not reflect their own concerns and interests. The TBT Committee plays an important role at this level. Nonetheless, developing countries do not participate enough in the committee's work.

Developing countries should participate in the standardization activities, and training programmes at international and national level. Developed countries must circulate the information at their disposal concerning regulations, standards and certification requirements among the exporters.

Technical regulations form a complex and vast corpus. The number of regulations and standards within the EU in 1988 was estimated at 100,000. They are continually increasing within the sphere of industry and high technology. Although regulations and standards do not deliberately constitute political measures, they may be motivated by geographical, biological and environmental considerations, and give rise to discrimination against the imported products. These specifications may be justified within the national context but can be inappropriate in another.

Box 3.1 Scallops (*pétoncles*) and scallop shells (*noix de saint Jacques*)

Some examples to illustrate how regulations may create barriers to trade. The law 100 in Quebec requires labels to be in French. This law constitutes a trade barrier in that it can discriminate against products coming from other Canadian provinces and other countries. At the moment, Quebec is pressing for labels to be written in good French. In 1993, France adopted a regulation that reserved the designation of 'noix de coquille Saint-Jacques'. It banned the import of Canadian coquille Saint Jacques under the pretext that they were different from the French variety. In 1994, the noix de Saint Jacques from Canada were labelled 'pétoncles' (their name in Quebec). Sales fell. This measure harmed Canadian interests, for exports represented a market of US$ 10 m. and 11 per cent of the French imports. Canada, supported by Peru and Chile, filed an action with the WTO because this obligation contravened Article 2 of the Agreement on Tariff Barriers, as well as Articles I and III of the GATT. At the WTO, this case was treated under the intellectual property register (appellation of origin).

Packaging and labelling

Packaging and labelling are part of the specifications that may create barriers to trade and are covered under the TBT Agreement.[2] National legislation on the elimination of waste or re-utilizable, recyclable or incinerable packaging may harm trade. Opinions on labelling depend on political persuasions. For some people, labels discriminate against foreign products and constitute real barriers to trade. For others, labelling improves the environmental performance of the products and encourages sustainable development. But labelling only represents a small part of environmental concerns. Generally speaking, the whole life cycle of a product starting with the extraction of raw materials and continuing with packaging has an impact on environment. Packaging, which represents an important part of the final cost of a product and may even be dearer than the product itself, has an important effect on the exports of developing countries. Packaging has to conform to the rules in force in a large number of countries.

Some of these rules relate to the collection of domestic waste after use. In France, the enterprise may employ the returnable system, a sub-contractor or use the services of the eco-packaging system. Requirements are similar in the Netherlands and in Germany, where the packaging enterprises or the importers are legally responsible for collecting the packaging.

In the United States, the system is complicated by a body of heterogeneous laws and regulations that govern the packaging system, and to which not all states subscribe. The 1990 'Clean Air Act' forbids products containing chlorofluorocarbons (CFCs) and hydro-chlorofluorocarbons (HCFCs). The law bans the sale of aerosol canisters and other synthetic packaging containing substances susceptible to having an effect on the ozone layer. Congress has, moreover, also legislated on drink containers through the National Beverage Container Reuse and Recycle Act of 1997.

Under pressure from the environmental movement, who comments that collection and re-utilization programmes have only limited success, accent is placed on the recycling of packaging rather than on their reuse. For non-food products, supply is concentrated on light packaging that facilitates reuse of the original receptacle. For logistic reasons, it is difficult to organize reusable packaging at an international level.

Labelling falls within the scope of Article 7 of the TBT Agreement. Eco-labelling may be obligatory if used to denote a toxic product. Other eco-labels are employed by producers to enhance their product and to take over a market in which there exists an environmental conscience. The labelling and eco-labelling may discriminate against an imported product. Environmental infrastructures differ according to the country (water purification plant, refuse incineration plant, and recycling plant). Supply of the materials and chemical components recommended by the labelled products may be difficult for foreign producers to obtain, especially in developing countries.

Since the late 1970s, more than twenty programmes have been adopted by the governments of developed countries, among them: *die Blaue Engel* for Germany; *Milieukeur* for the Netherlands; *Eco-brand* for Japan; *Green Seal* for the United States; *Norme française* (*NF*) for France; *Environment Canada* for Canada; the *Swan* for Norway; *Eco-label* for the EU and *Environmental Choice* for New Zealand. They are recognized by the ISO. The *Blaue Punkt* is a logo used by a German company as an indication that the waste will be recycled. Voluntary programmes exist in only a few developing countries (India,[3] Korea and Singapore). These programmes follow similar procedures. They inform the consumer about the environmental attributes of the products by favouring those selected by an official seal of approval. The consumer will thus recognize the environmental value of the product in relation to others that are similar.

These programmes, which have a national impact, have for some years become political instruments involving exports, especially in the fields of textiles and clothing, tropical timber, paper and wood pulp, the footwear industry, packaging in textiles (sisal and jute), and synthetics.

In developed countries, few products (about one hundred) are concerned with eco-labelling. Apart from certain sectors (detergents, food [bio products] and wood and derivatives), consumers do not yet systematically look for labelled products. But even if the extent of labelling and eco-labelling remains limited, this still has an effect on exports from developing countries, because they concern 'sensitive' goods, such as textiles and clothing, tropical timber, paper and wood pulp, and the footwear industry. Packaging in textile (sisal and jute), synthetic and paper material accounts for a considerable quantity of exports from developing countries (78.4 per cent, 20.9 per cent and 15 per cent, respectively).

In March 1992, the European Union adopted an eco-labelling plan for wood products. The environmental objectives pursued by this plan sought to favour recycled paper produced in Europe and the 'consumption of renewable resources', to the disadvantage of paper and wood pulp from Brazil. Denmark, which is responsible for the preparation of standards, does not distinguish between timber from sustainable development forests, and from other forests. They have opted for a definition concerning the management of sustainable forest, as a 'forest with many varieties of trees', which is not in international usage, and have ignored the fact that appreciable environmental results may be achieved by other means, and that solutions that are appropriate for Europe may be less so for other countries. Brazil and Canada, who employ other methods, have criticized this practice.

In 1992, the European Union adopted a regulation and programme for eco-labelling in the textile field. Once again, Denmark was entrusted with defining the criteria for obtaining T-shirts and cotton and polyester bed coverings. These criteria examined the methods by which cotton is produced (the use of pesticides, bio-acids, fertilizers and the way they are treated) and substances that have an effect on the ozone layer, such as waste water, printing, bleaching agents, detergent and auxiliary chemicals, dye products, and energy and water consumption.

The same conclusions may be drawn in the case of textiles as that of paper and wood pulp. The programme has discriminatory effects on international trade and penalizes exporting countries (especially Brazil). The programmes differ according to the country. Exporters must keep themselves informed of the current requirements for their export market and adapt their products according to each market. The first requirement is that of transparency. Importers must publish, inform and consult exporters before drawing up eco-labelling. ISO 14020 or 14040 have enacted standards for environmental systems and eco-labels.

The general rules for application that we have just discussed accompany rules that seek to neutralize the distorting effects caused by governmental policies, such as subsidies on agriculture, safeguarding measures, anti-dumping measures, rules on origin, investments, services, intellectual property rights and member state trading.

One of the most important Agreements discussed in the Uruguay Round was the Agreement on Agriculture, and this is discussed in Chapter 4.

4 The Agreement on Agriculture

Before the Uruguay Round, agriculture had been excluded from the considerable tariff reductions that had taken place during the previous negotiation rounds (the Dillon, Kennedy and Tokyo Rounds). Certain Articles in the GATT, moreover, allowed the employment of waivers in agricultural matters. Article XI 2 (c) of the GATT authorized the contracting parties to introduce tariff quotas when the countries were engaged in readjustments within the agricultural domain, or were attempting to reduce their production.

Certain countries were past masters in the art of protecting their market and obtaining waivers. During the Tokyo Round, two multilateral agreements had been concluded on beef and dairy products. The Agreement on Dairy Products was more restrictive for the participants than that on beef, on account of the introduction of a floor price that could not be exceeded. The clauses of the agreement were rapidly suspended. Few countries signed the agreements, which were therefore limited in their scope. Agriculture was eventually dealt with during the Uruguay Round.

Agriculture has caused real trade wars between the main producers. The United States has criticized the Common Agricultural Policy (CAP) of the European Union. Price support is central to the CAP, and is used as a production stimulus along with protective measures at the frontier employing a system of taxes on imports and export subsidies. This system gives off false signals to the producers concerning the given market opportunities.

The system induces surpluses of products such as milk powder, meat and wheat, which the EU seeks to dispose of on the world markets. The use of prices, through export subsidies (variable import levies and export refunds), causes distortions within world trade in agriculture. The CAP has caused serious profit losses for some agricultural exporting countries, especially the United States. The losses due to the fall in American exports have been estimated at $US65 million per annum since the 1960s. The dominant trading position of the United States in Portugal and Spain, where they held

50 per cent of the agricultural market in cereals and oilseeds, decreased with the entry of these countries into the EU in 1986.

Since the 1980s, the problem of the budgetary expense of the CAP, which had doubled since the mid-1970s and the 1980s, had been preoccupying the EU. The costs were reaching 70 per cent of the total EU expenses, and it was therefore necessary, either to reform the CAP, or to increase its budget – which was impossible in light of pressure from Great Britain. When the Uruguay Round negotiations started, the Community position remained as it had always been: that the CAP could not be challenged. Negotiations would only be possible subsequent to its reform in 1992 under the prompting of MacSharry, the Commissioner for Agriculture. Many countries considered the cost of agricultural subsidies to be too high, but the radical solution entailing the elimination of the subsidies was difficult to realize at the internal level because of the strong pressure from the agricultural lobbies. Negotiating the elimination of subsidies in a multilateral context, however, enabled the member states to overcome this impasse.

Despite the decline in agricultural trade, agriculture remains an important parameter of the social fabric. In the United States, agricultural interests are over-represented. The Iowa caucus is an obligatory step on the way to presidential nomination and all presidents have incorporated agricultural interests in their electoral platform. In most developed countries, the agricultural population does not exceed 6 per cent of the total active population, but in certain DCs (developing countries) and transition economies the figure is much higher – 26.7 per cent in Poland. In 1997, world trade in agriculture remained above 11 per cent of the world trade in goods, exceeding that of cars, textile products and oil. Agricultural trade plays a more important role in the economic activity of developing countries than in that of developed countries, especially in Latin America and Africa. But these countries nevertheless have difficulties in transforming this importance into a larger market share of the world market in agricultural products. Between 1980 and 1997, these remained stable.

The Agreement on Agriculture: objectives and main characteristics

The new rules and engagements negotiated in the area of agriculture during the Uruguay Round, especially the undertaking to restart the negotiations towards the end of 1999, were designated collectively under the name of the Reform Programme, stemming from the Uruguay Round. This programme formed the first step of a longer-term process that aimed, through substantial and progressive reductions in support and protection, to set up a system of trade in agricultural products that was both equitable and market-oriented.

The agreement not only reflected trade concerns, but certain of its provisions were related to food safety[1] export restrictions and to the Agreement on Sanitary and Phytosanitary Measures. In addition, developing and less advanced countries benefited from special and differentiated treatment. The considerations relating to trade concerned commitments on market access, internal support, export subsidies and import credits. Article 20, based on the first results from implementing the commitments on trade in agricultural products, envisaged the continuation of the reform process.

All the customs duties relating to agricultural products were to be consolidated and reduced. From the point of view of the developed countries before the Uruguay Round, 58 per cent of the tariff lines were consolidated, 51 per cent for transition countries and only 18 per cent for developing countries. It was the latter who had to make the greatest effort in entirely consolidating their tariff line in relation to agriculture.

The non-tariff barriers, for which the agreement provided a non-exhaustive list, contained quantitative restrictions, variable levies, discretionary import regimes, and measures instituted by state-run trading enterprises that corresponded to a non-tariff barrier were converted into equivalent tariffs (tariffication) that were consolidated and reduced in their turn. Because of this, Article XI 2 (c) of the GATT became unusable.

Market access, internal supports and export subsidies: the three pillars of the agreement

With respect to market access, tariffication was one of the most important aspects of the Agreement on Agriculture. The tariff equivalent of the non-tariff measures had been calculated on the basis of the average world prices of the product, subject to non-tariff measures, and their guaranteed prices in the importing countries during the 1986–1988 base period. The calculation was left to the care of each member, but was subject to a verification process and consultations between the interested parties in December 1993 and April 1994 (1995 for developing countries).

Developed countries had to reduce their tariffs by 36 per cent during an implementation period of six years, and developing countries by 24 per cent over a period of ten years. Less advanced countries were not required to reduce their tariffs, but to consolidate them.

Tariffication sometimes gave rise to prohibitive tariffs that did not correspond to the market opportunities before the Uruguay Round. Quotas enable this drawback to be mitigated by authorizing the import of a certain volume at reduced duties in connection with the consolidated non-quota rate. Once the quota is reached, the higher tariff applies. The tariffs applicable under quotas and non-quotas, as well as the quota volumes, are consolidated and recorded in the concession lists of each member. Some thirty-six countries (including Morocco, Tunisia and South Africa) have started tariff quotas amounting to 1,370. According to UNCTAD, quotas do not really offer real access to markets, because they are granted selectively by the importing countries.

Thirty-eight member countries have the possibility of resorting to the special safeguard clause (Article 5) in order to impose an additional duty on a temporary basis to agricultural products designated 'SGS' on their list. The provisions may be invoked in the case of a sudden increase in the volume of the imports with regard to the existing access possibilities over the three previous years, or when the import price CIF of a consignment falls below the average reference price recorded during the period 1986–1988. The special safeguard measures can only be applied on a customs duty associated with the tariffication of a non-tariff measure. The question that arises is how to know whether this clause will be temporary or permanent.

All WTO members have made commitments concerning the internal support that they grant their agricultural producers, whether at the national or the infra-national level, in the form of undertakings to reduce the internal support registered in lists (the 'consolidated annual and final levels of commitment', indicated in Section I of Part IV of the lists of a certain number of WTO members), and general commitments resulting from the rules concerning: (1) three categories of support measures not forming the subject of a reduction according to the agreement, and (2) the support not exceeding the stipulated *de minimis* levels.

For this reason, the agreement does not prohibit internal support. It does, however, classify internal support according to its distorting effect on international trade, thus encouraging countries to modify their agricultural policy by employing measures that have no distorting effect on trade and production. Three categories were thus created. The first category is that of the 'Green Box' whose effects on trade or production are nil, or at most minimal, and that conform to the basic and specific criteria laid down in the agreement. The latter provides a non-exhaustive list of these measures.[2]

The direct payments, by way of production limitation programmes, that meet the requirements set out in Paragraph 5 of Article 6 are part of the 'Blue Box'. This category includes direct payments that are 'partly uncoupled', but, in benefiting from such payments, producers must not be encouraged to increase the volume of their production.[3]

Residual support measures of the 'orange and yellow' category that do not belong to the three above-mentioned categories are generally methods of support by product, such as market price support and non-exempted direct payments, and all other non-exempted measures and subsidies, such as input subsidies and measures for the reduction of marketing costs.

No upper limit has been fixed by way of support for these three categories, but all new or modified green, S&D (special and differential treatment) and blue categories must be notified as rapidly as possible to the Agricultural Committee. Developing countries have considerable flexibility at their disposal in applying internal support measures, since they are authorized to undertake aid to the agricultural sector within the scope of the S&D category, even if these are coupled to agricultural production, investment subsidies, financing of agricultural inputs for low-income producers, or diversification programmes for the abandonment of illicit crops.

In conformity with the provisions on the *de minimis* levels of Article 6.4 of the agreement, reduction of the residual orange category is not required if it does not exceed, over a year, 5 per cent (10 per cent for developing countries) of the value of the total production (in the case of support by product) of the initial agricultural product concerned, or by the total value of agricultural production in the case of support other than by product. The *de minimis* clause therefore enables all countries to use forms of subsidies that are not exempted from reduction commitments, in as far as they do not exceed the ceilings intended for developing countries (10 per cent) and for developed countries (5 per cent). The orange category support, which is lower than the *de minimis* ceiling, by product and other than by product, may be raised to these levels, although this may have an effect on the possibility or not of giving rise to an action within Article 13 (b) of the peace clause.

Commitments for the reduction of internal support apply to all internal support measures in favour of agricultural producers. These commitments are expressed in monetary terms by means of a global support measure (GSM) and are consolidated. The calculation methods set up for each agricultural product as well as for the non-specific supports for products are specified in the annex to the agreement.[4]

According to the peace clause or 'due restraint clause' (Article 13 of the agreement), the category green measures, which are fully in conformity with the basic and fixed criteria according to the measures set forth in Annex 2: (1) do not give rise to an action with a view to applying for compensatory rights; (2) are not exempt from actions on account of serious prejudice by way of the WTO Agreement on Subsidies; and (3) are exempt from actions founded upon the annulment or reduction, in a situation of non-violation, of the advantages of the tariff concessions. The fact that category green subsidies do not give rise to an action is one of the characteristics that distinguish the exempted measures of S&D categories and Blue Box.

As regards the Blue and S&D Boxes, the possibility of instituting proceedings under Article VI of the 1994 GATT and under the Agreement on Subsidies depends on establishing the existence of prejudice caused in conformity with the normal provisions of the GATT/WTO, and of the moderation shown in the opening of any enquiry regarding compensatory rights. In this respect, the basic provisions set forth in Part V of the SCM (subsidies and compensatory measures) Agreement, especially concerning the consultations with the interested exporting member envisaged in Article 13, would be fully respected.

Similarly, the exemptions from the possibility of giving rise to an action set forth in paras (ii) and (iii) of Article 13 (b), are both subordinate to the fact that the measures in question concerning internal support do not grant support for a specific product that exceeds the amount that was decided during the 1992 marketing programme (very probably in the national legislation).

All export subsidies that were distorting the international trade in agricultural products are excluded by the agreement, inclusive of those enumerated in Article 9. The 'other' export subsidies are treated in Article 10 of the agreement, according to which, export subsidies not enumerated in Article 9.1 shall not be applied in a way that leads, or threatens to lead to a circumvention of the commitments regarding export subsidies. The agreement envisages two exceptions. Only those member countries that have incorporated reduction commitments in Part IV of their list can call upon export subsidies within the limits recorded in their lists. The lists designate the products for which the members have the right to pay export subsidies, and determine, for each product, the reductions to be undertaken, both at the level of the volume exported and of the amounts of the budgetary expenses. Products not specified on the lists may not benefit from subsidies (zero commitment).

Reductions must be made on the volume exported and on the budgetary expenses. Developed countries must reduce their expenses devoted to export subsidies by 36 per cent in six equal stages spread over six years (in relation to 1986–1990 levels). The volume of subsidized exports must also be reduced by 21 per cent in six equal stages extending over six years, relative to the same base period.

For developing countries, the percentage reductions are 24 per cent and 14 per cent respectively, and they must be carried out in equal annual stages over ten years. In future, no export subsidy can be granted for products that are not subject to reduction commitments of these subsidies. Article 9.2 (b) envisages certain flexibility in fulfilling commitments between the second year (1996) and the fifth year (1999) of the implementation period. If the effective expenses or the quantities accumulated do not reach the appropriate annual levels of commitment, the amount may, under certain limits, be carried over to the following fulfilment period. This clause, however, which involves a certain number of economic risks, has been criticized by members.[5] It can only be to the advantage of countries that are financially able to resort to it, and it creates artificial market conditions.[6]

The second exception concerns developing countries. According to Article 9.4, these are not held to reduction commitments in the case of subsidies destined to reduce the marketing costs of agricultural products, and, in the case of preferential tariffs, for the internal transport of goods intended for export under more favourable conditions than for consignments in internal trade. This exception is restricted to the implementation period of the agreement, a period of six years commencing in 1995 (Article 1 (f)). Developing countries, moreover, may not use this temporary exception in order to exceed the commitment levels recorded on their list.

The agreement envisages a reduction in export subsidies. These subsidies are especially important in the case of heavily subsidized products, such as wheat, secondary cereals, dairy products and sugar. From now till the end of the period, the total amount of export subsidies of agricultural products will be reduced from US$22,500 billion to US$14,500 billion, and half of this reduction will be attributable to the European Union.

As commitments to reduce export subsidies continue, pressures in favour of a wider resort to other forms of export assistance could increase. The utilization of 'other' export subsidies is prohibited according to the anti-circumvention provisions of Article 10.1, which aims not only at subsidized credits and allied facilities, but also 'non-trade transactions', including food aid.

In the case of subsidized credits, some work has already been undertaken by the OECD. As regards transactions concerning food aid, Article 10.4 establishes a certain number of specific obligations aimed at reinforcing existing commitments or procedural regulations adopted by other international bodies that are specifically responsible for questions relative to food aid or the disposal of surpluses. In general, international food aid must not be directly or indirectly allied to commercial transactions, must be carried out in conformity with the appropriate FAO or Sustainable Development Commission procedures, and only transactions relevant to international food aid that conform to Article IV of the International Food Aid Convention will be considered to be 'international food aid' for the purposes of the Agreement on Agriculture.

In addition, Article IV of this convention ('Food aid contribution methods') lays down that food aid may be provided in any of the following ways: gifts; cash contributions to be employed for financing food aid to the advantage of the beneficiary country; the sale of cereals against money of the beneficiary country that is not convertible into currency or goods and services capable of being used by the donor country; and credit sales of products constituting food aid, with payment by reasonable annuities spread over twenty years or more, at an interest rate below the prevailing commercial rates on the world markets. Transactions not carried out according to this method would have to be integrated within the limits of the commitment levels. In fact, almost all food aid now comes in the form of gifts.

Export subsidies that are completely in conformity with the Agreement on Agriculture are exempt from actions based on Article XVI of the 1994 GATT or Article 3 (prohibition of export subsidies) and Articles 5 and 6 (serious prejudice) of the Agreement on Subsidies. The fact that a measure may not give rise to an action under the Agreement on Subsidies is not linked to the amount or degree of internal support that is granted for a specific product in relation to what it had been during the 1992 marketing campaign.

The committee must review the level of international food aid, within the terms of the FAO Convention, in order to assess the food problems and financial import problems of developing countries that are net importers of foodstuffs. It must enter into negotiations with the FAO in order to maintain a level of commitment suitable for satisfying their food needs. The FAO Convention is undergoing reforms in order to extend the list of products covered and involve more countries. Finally, it must adopt guidelines in order for food aid to be given in the shape of gifts or favourable concessions to developing countries.

Countries engaged in reduction commitments must notify the Agriculture Committee every year regarding market access, their tariff or other quotas and special safeguard clauses, and, in matters of internal support, their total current GSM (global support measures) and new or modified exempted measures, as well as their subsidies and export restrictions. Members must follow the explicit directives with regard to the frequency and presentation of the notifications.

As regards tariff quotas, all changes must be subject to specific notifications, normally presented before the opening of the quota, but, in any case, 30 days at the latest after this date. Notification of changes should be carried out, wherever possible before the change has been introduced, but in any case 30 days at the latest after the change.

Members must also undertake an annual notification after the end of the calendar year (or financial year, marketing campaign, etc.) in question, indicating the imports that have been the subjected to tariff and other quotas. All members who have reserved the right of recourse to the special safeguard clause (Article 5 of the Agreement on Agriculture) in their lists must notify them.

The Agriculture Committee examines in depth the reduction commitments of the members and ensures the correct observation of the new regulations on the trade in agricultural products. In performing its first task it has three main tools: (1) notifications received from all member countries; (2) counter-notifications that enable every member to make known to the Committee any measure that in the member's opinion should have been notified by another member; and (3) questions raised during the Committee meetings relating to implementation problems encountered by any member country.

The Agreement on Agriculture and developing countries

At the commitment level, developing countries have the advantage of lower reductions than those that are carried out by developed countries on market access (two-thirds of those carried out on market access, internal support measures and export subsidies), and benefit from longer transition periods.

Developing countries and those in transition have confirmed reductions in customs duties that they have already adopted unilaterally, either by consolidating at lower rates or by rate ceilings. These customs duties are expected to decrease further, in certain cases even beyond the reductions agreed in the Uruguay Round, following additional liberalization measures that a certain number of countries have taken or envisage taking, in order to promote growth directed towards export.

The WTO notification system is cumbersome. Up to now, the Committee has received little information on behalf of developing countries. The less advanced countries are nevertheless not required to notify their internal support measures every year, but can do so every two years. Moreover, they have no commitments, to reduce export subsidies and internal support measures. But they must, however, send information to the committee, although in a simplified form.

Developing countries, especially the African countries, often wonder about the impact of the agreement on the structure of the trade preferences that have been granted to them by the EU. Within the context of the new negotiations, the main problem that the DC (developing countries) have is to know whether the negotiating capital at their disposal will be spent more appropriately in the negotiations on the supplementary tariff reductions or in extending preferential tariffs. There is no doubt, however, that the method chosen – of opting for tariffs – is more promising, because it is likely that the WTO will follow this path. Developing countries have an interest in participating in the liberalization of trade, by ensuring that their products are incorporated, rather than opting out.

Their interests may diverge, but convergence also exists. Developed countries have pursued distorting practices that have harmed developing countries, but certain developing countries have themselves adopted high agricultural tariffs as a result of protectionist practices inherited from the past. Many DC, moreover, use para-state agencies for the marketing and control of foodstuffs, and these have often hindered their economic development. DC have every interest in continuing the liberalization process that they have already started.

A reduction or elimination of agricultural support in industrialized countries may contribute to stimulating agricultural production and exports of African countries. In the short and medium term, however, food prices are going to rise because of the decrease of agricultural production in developed countries. This price rise will probably increase pressure on the balance of payment of many importers of agricultural products and have consequences for their debt. Following a rise in the price of foodstuffs during the first year of implementation, prices of foodstuffs fell.

Food aid has fallen since 1994 and export receipts to cover their imports have themselves fallen. Action must therefore be taken to improve DCs' ability to pay for agricultural imports that are necessary for their food supply while strengthening their agricultural production.

Despite the advantages represented by the agreement, the quantitative benefits that DC derive from it have not materialized. At access to markets level, agricultural tariffs remain much higher than industrial tariffs. Their average is 32.4 per cent as against 5.7 per cent for industrial products. Other points to note on tariffs are:

- Tariffs are equivalent to non-tariff measures, or 'dirty tariffication' used by member countries. Thirty-eight developed countries are over-valued, to an amount equivalent to that of 100 per cent tariffs. Levels of protection are higher than the measures that the tariffication replaced. There are harmful tariff peaks for many DC products, such as sugar, tobacco and cotton. Reductions already carried out have been imposed on the lowest tariffs and tariff quotas have not been completely utilized: 65 per cent in 1995, 63 per cent in 1996 and 46 per cent in 1997.
- Certain countries, including developed countries and the Cairns Group, think that the criteria used to define the Green Box are too broad, and enable countries to conceal internal support measures that do not fulfil the Green Box principles. Only a few countries have reduced export subsidies: six countries have employed 75 per cent of the reduction commitment, and the DC proportion is 20 per cent.

  Following tariffication of agricultural non-tariff measures under the WTO agreement, the simple average EU tariff in 1995 across all products, agricultural and manufacturing, has been estimated at 9.6 per cent; this is a notional increase compared to the 7.3 per cent prior to the Round, but is explained by the conversion of non-tariff measures to tariffs (tariffication) in agriculture rather than an increase in the overall level or protection (Auboin and Laird 1997: 3). The new tariffs show peaks for meat and meat products, dairy products, sugar and derivatives, and tobacco products.

Towards future negotiations

The text of Article 20 of the Agreement on Agriculture authorizes the continuation of the reform process. The concept of multifunctionality, which first appeared at the Rio de Janeiro Summit, is central to the position and negotiation strategy of the EU. Article 20 stipulates that negotiations should take account of non-commercial preoccupations, but does not explicitly mention multifunctionality. Multifunctionality includes nutrition, safeguarding, management and improvement of the rural environment, the protection of human beings, animals and plants, and consumer concerns.[7]

Multifunctionality has become the European cultural model and is employed as the fourth negotiation pillar alongside internal support, export subsidies and the S&D treatment for developing countries. It could thus give rise to inter-sectoral offsetting. But the concept remains vague, and this could indeed be useful, especially during the negotiations. Few countries disagree that agriculture not only concerns the production of food and that it comprises other functions, including non-commercial objectives.

The EU has found allies. Thirty-four countries have rallied to the concept, including those in development, and countries such as South Korea, Japan, Norway and Switzerland that practise subsidized agriculture, and Central and East European countries that have been quick to align themselves with the EU. The WTO does not oppose the concept as long as it does not create distortions within international trade.

The origins of multifunctionality go back to 1982. Many member states were worried by the changes that had come about in the European countryside and by pollution. The Green Paper on the future of agriculture proposed that greater account should be taken of environmental policy and the following of practices that are more consistent with environmental protection. According to Skogstad, the Commission reflected on the role of agriculture in preserving the countryside in order to restore the tarnished image of the CAP. The non-governmental organizations play a not unimportant role in this respect.

The CAP reform introduced offsetting agro-environmental payments for disadvantaged regions and income support for farmers who followed practices that respected the environment. The introduction of direct payments in the CAP enabled rural society to be preserved, and rural development became an integral part of rural development in the 2000 agenda, introduced in 1997 and in the second pillar of the CAP. In addition, the

Amsterdam Treaty that came into force in May 1999 made the Community responsible for including environmental considerations in all legislation.

The leitmotif of the Commission resides in the necessity for the agricultural sector to maintain rural society and activity. Food safety and environmental protection cannot be ensured solely by market forces (Franz Fischler, speech delivered on 1 July 2000). Production-linked payments are essential to obtain the desired production.

Subsidies are at the heart of the problem. The United States and the Cairns Group maintain that multifunctionality risks deviating from the discipline relative to subsidies and may justify other objectives, including protectionism. The Blue Box and Green Box subsidies are the principal items of discussion. The Blue Box could disappear during the next negotiations.[8] Some effort should be made to reinforce discipline with the Green Box, in order to reduce the possibilities of circumvention.

Member states are exerting pressure for the inclusion of environmental issues in the Blue and Green Boxes. The EU seeks to show that Blue Box payments are very useful instruments, whereas the United States and the Cairns Group would like to eliminate them. The EU has adopted a stand-off position in order to avoid being confined within pre-established categories.

The United States is seeking improved access for its products subject to quotas (cereals, soya beans, beef, poultry and citrus fruits), including their biotechnological products, and greater discipline for state enterprises, as well as the banning of export subsidies.

The United States wants the Blue Box to be eliminated. They are supported by the Cairns Group, which maintains that multifunctionality does not apply to agriculture, since the Green Box is sufficiently flexible to adjust to non-commercial considerations. Environmental protection can be covered by subsidies directed exclusively towards the environment. Export subsidies have led to a fall in international prices and forced farmers to produce the best possible market for ensuring greater profits – a procedure that is not the most respectful of the environment.

Switzerland is acting as an arbitrator between the EU and the United States. It recognizes that certain members can justify their excessive protection by the need to preserve the non-commercial effects of agriculture. On the other hand, reduction of product supports and the liberalization of trade could provoke a decline in agricultural services beneath the socially required level. Conciliation of these points of view constitutes the greatest challenge for the negotiations.

The supporters of multifunctionality demand that the WTO should be more flexible and permit governments to pursue the policies of their choice. They maintain that the Green Box measures are insufficient to satisfy environmental concerns. Many countries, especially those in development, consider that these proposals would result in granting developed countries S&D treatment (http:/www.wto.org).

Agricultural negotiations: converging or diverging interests?

Many issues are going to influence the agricultural negotiations, including those concerning intellectual property and the Agreement on Sanitary and Phytosanitary Measures. Other considerations, such as state trading, quota administration, export restrictions and the preference system should also be a part of the negotiations. Table 4.1 offers an overview of these matters.

Intellectual property has an effect on the agricultural and food sectors, in the domain of inputs and seeds. So-called 'terminator' technology or sterile seeds worry farmers, because they have to pay for their seeds every season. It is therefore absolutely essential to reach an agreement that would enable research to continue, but without extorting excessive profits from intellectual property rights.

GMO (genetically modified organisms) are increasingly employed in developed countries, and the question has become a crucial one in many countries. Some 55 per cent of the soya cultivated in the United States is transgenic and 35 per cent of the wheat. The United States are the greatest users of GMO, with 20.5 million ha. planted, followed by 4.3 in Argentina, 2.8 in Canada and 0.1 in Australia (Table 4.2). GMO already constitute a not unimportant part of agricultural trade. It is certain that the use of GMO contributes to increasing harvests (35 per cent) and reducing the use of herbicides (15–29 per cent). The position of the countries depends on how they evaluate the danger of GMO to public health. The United States has filed a complaint against the EU at the WTO.

The EU has embarked on a policy of reducing its agricultural expenses, whereas the United States is increasing its. The two partners could find a

Table 4.1 Agricultural issues on the negotiation agenda

Main issues	*New issues*	*Parallel issues*
Market access	TRQ (tariff rate quota)	Preference schemes
Export subsidies	Export restrictions	
Internal support	State trading	Intellectual property, sanitary and phytosanitary measures, competition policy

Source: Josling and Tangermann (1999).

Table 4.2 Sown surfaces involving GMO

Country	Area planted (million hectares)
USA	20.5
Argentina	4.3
Canada	2.8
Australia	0.1
Mexico	0.1
Spain	0.1
France	0.1
South Africa	0.1
Total	27.8

common ground. The United States has damped down their criticisms of multifunctionality, but its definition of it is more precise. For the United States, multifunctionality comprises food security, resource conservation, rural development and environmental protection. They fear the involvement of multifunctionality in subsidies and trade distortion. A range of instruments contained in the Green Box is capable of answering environmental concerns without causing distortions.

Are negotiations more difficult now than ten years ago? Negotiators employ a common language and methodology. The United States and the EU can find ground for agreement. Export subsidies remain the only problem (in fact the United States and the EU finally reached an agreement in July 2004).

Agricultural negotiations and the new round of negotiations

Economic negotiations form a complex body of multilateral agreements, negotiated separately by several countries. The accent in these negotiations is on solving problems and maximizing the trade-off between the issues (Zartman 1986: 285). These trade-offs are encouraged by the number of issues (ibid.). Thanks to a full agenda, all the issues were discussed together and the number of combinations and links – and consequently the number of trade-offs and negotiation packages – have been maximized (Jönsson 1978: 38). Thus, as Homans affirmed (1961): "when many issues are obligatory for the negotiators, the chances of reaching a conclusion are greater". The parties to the negotiation are able to change subjects to their mutual benefit.

The Uruguay Round was interlocked with specific and functional issues that were of mutual advantage to the countries. The structure of the negotiations offered the possibility of trade-offs between the different parties. The internal structure of the subjects also helped the negotiations. Services comprising several domains – tourism, professional services, communications, education, health, financial and transport services – could be negotiated separately. To secure concessions in ocean transport by developing countries, developed countries made counter-proposals on liberalizing non-qualified personnel.

Agriculture would attract greater attention in the new round of negotiations if they extended to services and agriculture. On the other hand, the probability of obtaining more reductions in the agricultural negotiations would be greater if the agenda of the negotiations included several sectors. This would enable non-agricultural groups to participate and exert pressure on the negotiations in order to obtain advantages in other areas of negotiation. This was the same in the Uruguay Round when German industrial pressure groups mobilized in order to bring a halt to the agricultural procrastinations. In 1991, the German government was faced by worker demonstrations demanding the cessation of the negotiations.

Another important Agreement is the General Agreement on Trade in Services (GATS), and this is discussed in Chapter 5.

5 The General Agreement on Trade in Services (GATS)

The Agreement on Services is the first multilateral agreement aimed at liberalizing services, which are becoming increasingly commercialized. Hitherto considered as support for the trade in goods, services are now recognized as also being negotiable products. Liberalizing services permits this sector to be modernized through the contribution of foreign investments, but also benefits the whole economy. In the mid-1980s, the trade in services represented nearly one-fifth of world exports, and its share of added value was 37 per cent for low-income countries, 53 per cent for middle-income countries and more than 70 per cent for developed countries (Stephenson 2000: 3).

Developed countries are the main exporters of services (75 per cent), followed by developing countries (21 per cent), and then by transition economies (4 per cent). The United States, Japan and the EU are the main users, purveyors and exporters of services. In developed countries, services may represent as much as 60 per cent of the GNP. In the United States, they account for 80 per cent of the GNP, and in Korea and Brazil, respectively, represent 50 per cent and 64 per cent of the GNP.

The United States is dominant in transport, telecommunications, computers and information, followed by Great Britain, Japan and Canada. Great Britain is paramount in insurance, followed by Canada, the United States and Italy. The United States and Great Britain are leaders in financial services. Among the ten outstanding world exporters are some developing countries such as Hong Kong, Brazil, Singapore and China. In the small and medium countries of Latin America and the Caribbean, exports of services constitute the major part of their foreign currency and employment.

Developing countries possess comparative advantages in services, and some of them have found niches that ensure them a large part of the market. India is a leader in computers, for example. Certain sectors offer many potentialities for developing countries, such as for professional and business services (computers and office machinery), health, tourism, construction, audiovisual services and transport. Cuba, India and Jordan have developed their health services, and the costs of a coronary by-pass are now lower in India than in the United States.

Several pharmaceutical companies have concluded agreements in India for the construction of polyclinics. SERVIMED is a company set up in Cuba to offer health/tourism packages. During the years 1995/1996, 25,000 patients and 1,500 students went to Cuba for treatment or study. Profits amounted to US$25 million.

India, Malaysia and Taiwan have undertaken research and development activities in order to promote their office machinery sector. India, Bangalore and New Delhi have developed computer support services employing 25,000 people, and software exports have grown in this way from US$225 million in 1992–1993 to US$2,700 million per annum in 1999. British Airways and Swissair have a whole series of computer data processed in the Bangalore and Poona centres.

Except for some sectors, such as maritime transport, services are neither tangible nor can they be stored, and are not subject to duties at the frontier. On the other hand, the public authorities quite strictly regulate services. These regulations frequently discriminate against foreign suppliers through the adoption of a whole variety of technical standards. These are not imposed so much on the product as upon the sectors and the producer. The legal consolidation of the operating conditions that must offset the absence of customs duties is an important aspect of the agreement.

In point of fact, unlike access to markets relating to the delivery of goods from one country to another (which essentially concerns the question of customs duties and other formalities at the frontier), the ability to supply a service to another country depends largely on the official regulations in force there, and these may differ quite considerably. A doctor or a hairdresser who sets up in a foreign country pays no customs duties but he/she must be able to benefit from 'national treatment' in order to operate freely.

Unlike goods, which circulate physically from one country to another, trade in services does not necessarily involve a cross-border movement. Certain services, however, require the supplier and consumer of the services to be in the same place at the same time, or for the consumer to go to the country where the services are offered.

Services: negotiation process

In the United States, the private sector – especially the financial sector – has exerted pressure on the American administration to enable the service sector in Asia to be liberalized and the capital of the companies to be controlled. When, during the 1982 GATT Ministerial Conference, the United States proposed that the contracting parties should consider services, they encountered considerable opposition from the EU, Japan, Canada and Switzerland. After carrying out national studies, however, certain developed countries – such as those in the EU – sided with the United States. Opposition came principally from developing countries, such as Brazil, Egypt, India, Argentina, the former Yugoslavia and Tanzania, which were opposed to the inclusion of services in the negotiations.

Developing countries were afraid of being compelled to negotiate services to the detriment of other dossiers that were of higher priority to them, such as agriculture, textiles, tariff ceilings and safeguard clauses. They felt that overloading the negotiations with new issues could be harmful to their interests, and they did not want the GATT rules, particularly on national treatment, to be applied to the services sector. They also feared losing control of an important sector of the economy that was in full expansion.

But these positions gradually lost their edge in favour of a convergence between the positions held by the developed and developing countries. The more moderate group of developing countries were apprehensive of having to pay too high a price in other negotiation sectors if they did not give ground on services.

A compromise was reached during the Punta del Este meeting in September 1986. Brazil and India agreed to a proposal that no longer opposed the inclusion of services during the negotiations. The structure of the negotiations reflected the proposals put forward by the developing countries, notably by the Latin American and African countries. Access to markets and national treatment were not commitments but a matter of negotiation. Developing countries obtained a progressive opening of their markets.

The Agreement on Trade in Services (AGCS): main characteristics

The AGCS aimed at the expansion of trade in services and national economies, as well as a growing participation by developing countries. It identified twelve principal areas of activity: services provided by enterprises; communication services; construction and associated engineering services; distribution; education; energy; environmental affairs; financial services; health and social services; services relating to tourism and travel; recreational, cultural and sports services; and services allied to transport (WTO Secretariat 2001). In principle, this is simple, but procedurally it is complex. In its general structure and also to a certain extent in its content, the entire results of the Uruguay Round concerning services resemble all the provisions applied to goods. The fundamental principles of the GATT, such as 'national treatment', non-discrimination, and transparency, apply to the agreement. Even so, a certain resemblance may lead to confusion. The principle of national treatment, for example, is fundamental to the GATS just as it is to the GATT, but it is applied in a very different way. In the GATS it is operative unless the commitment list does not indicate to the contrary. There is no obligation, however, to offer national treatment and market access to foreign suppliers.

The agreement comprises twenty-nine articles (thirty-two if the three additional articles are counted separately), annexes and commitment lists of the countries (*schedules*), comprising exemption lists. The agreement contains six parts. The introductory part sets out the scope and definition of the agreement. Part II, which is the longest, deals with obligations and disciplines, such as the rules applying for the most part to all services and members (the MFN clause, national treatment and transparency). Part III sets out the rules governing the specific commitments filed in the lists. Part IV concerns future negotiations and the lists themselves. Parts V and VI detail the institutional and final provisions. Three essential articles form the basis of the agreement. Article VI deals with national regulations, and specifies that each member state must ensure that its general application measures are applied in a reasonable, objective and impartial way. Article XVI lists the measures as different types of quotas, which may not be filed in the commitment lists unless they have been designated, and Article XVII prohibits any discriminatory treatment of foreign services and providers of services (Feketekuty 2000).

Services that are 'provided in the exercise of the governmental authority' are excluded from the agreement (justice, police, diplomacy, currency, prisons and fire fighting), the latter of course being services that are not provided on a commercial basis. Education and health are covered by the agreement since private schools and hospitals exist side by side with public schools and private clinics. The document also covers all measures affecting the trade in services conducted, and by all the public authorities (central governments and administrations, local and regional governments, and non-governmental organizations under public authority mandate).

Article I contains a detailed definition of the trade in services according to four modes of delivering the services. This may be:

- *cross-border* – possibility for non-resident service providers in one country to provide services across the frontier on the territory of another member state (telephonic communication or maritime transport);
- *consumption abroad* – freedom for the residents of one member state to purchase the services in the territory of another;
- *commercial presence*[1] – possibilities for foreign providers of services to set up, manage or establish a commercial presence, such as an agency

or subsidiary in another member territory. This presence encompasses all types of businesses or establishments whose aim is to provide a service.

* *presence of physical persons* – possibilities granted to foreign persons for admission and temporary residence in the territory of the member state, in order to provide a service (as consultant, for example).

Commitments relating to some 150 different forms of service activity were recorded in the lists filed by the member states. Certain services can be provided by several of the four modes, whereas others – by their very nature – cannot be.[2]

Part II stipulates the 'obligations and general disciplines'. This concerns the basic rules that apply to all members, and mostly to all services. Article II of the GATS, relative to the treatment of the most favoured nation, thus relates directly to the first Article of the GATT. In accordance with its first paragraph, 'concerning all measures covered by the present agreement each Member shall immediately and unconditionally accord the services and service providers of every Member a treatment no less favourable than that which it accords to a similar service or service provider of any other country'.

Apart from the services specified in the various lists of exemptions from the MFN commitment, the only case where it is permitted to deviate from the most favoured nation treatment within the scope of the GATS is when countries are members of economic integration agreements.[3] By virtue of Article V, every member of the WTO has the right to conclude an agreement for the increased liberalization of trade in services exclusively with other parties to the agreement and in dispensation of the MFN clause, on condition that the agreement covers a substantial number of sectors, eliminates or excludes measures that introduce discrimination against providers of services from other countries of the group, and does not create new barriers to trade. Article V relates to Article XXIV of the 1994 GATT. It suffers, however, from the same deficiencies as Article XXIV, in that there is a lack of clarity regarding the interpretation of the conditions for the application of Article V.[4]

The classical affirmation of the MFN principle is moderated in the Agreement on Services. Members are permitted to maintain a measure incompatible with the general MFN commitment, as long as they have notified it. The lists of exemptions are regulated by the conditions set down in an annex to the GATS. The agreement clearly establishes that no new exemptions can be granted except for maritime transport and for countries in the process of accession to the WTO. The exemptions filed in the lists are subject to a specified time limit. For those that are not, the Annex envisages that they should not in principle continue for more than ten years (i.e. not beyond 2004).

Article XVI (access to markets) draws up an exhaustive list of conditions for access to markets and enumerates four kinds of quantitative restrictions (paras a. to d.), as well as the limitations concerning the form of legal entity (para. e.) and the participation of foreign capital (para. f.). This list also embraces measures that could be discriminatory in respect of national treatment (Article XVII) and involves the number of service providers, whether in the form of numerical quotas, monopolies, exclusive suppliers or from the requirement for an analysis of economic needs. The limitations also concern the total value of the transactions or assets relating to the services, in the form of numerical quotas or the requirement for an examination of economic needs.

The second basic principle adopted from the GATT is that of transparency. The agreement requires members to publish, in the shortest possible time, all pertinent measures for general application, and to notify the Council for Trade in Services of laws, regulations or directives affecting them. Every member must establish an information point for dealing with requests for information from other members.

With regard to developing countries, the most developed of them must set up contact points where service providers interested in developing countries can obtain information about the availability of service technologies, commercial aspects and techniques for supplying services, recording, and the recognition and acquisition of professional qualifications. Developing countries have additional time extensions beyond the requisite two years for setting up these contact points.

Other rules are included in Part II in order to ensure that national regulations do not impede the advantages arising from the agreement. Article VII recommends regimes for unilateral, bilateral or multilateral recognition. The harmonization of the regulations is a prerequisite for mutual recognition, and the agreement recommends the establishment of cooperation and an exchange of data and analysis of the regulations in order to satisfy the principle of mutual recognition. NAFTA and the EU harmonized the national regulations before confirming mutual recognition (Nicolaidis 2000: 43–71).

The agreement invites members to recognize qualifications (academic and others) of service providers from other countries. The agreement authorizes governments to conclude bilateral or multilateral arrangements for the mutual recognition of certificates, licences and other authorizations (Article VII), and encourages members who have concluded such agreements to grant the same opportunities to every other member. The most favoured nation clause does not apply to the recognition of qualifications.

The only requirements are those of transparency and the possibility of negotiating similar recognition agreements. France offers nationals from African countries the right to carry on professions that is not offered to other countries.

Service providers are not authorized to act in a way that is incompatible with the MFN obligations of a member or with its specific commitments, or to take advantage of its monopolistic position. Such practices are not, however, penalized. The agreement only recommends that members and service providers may consult one another when they are faced by a lack of competition. Article VIII recommends that monopolies closed to foreign providers shall not take unfair advantage of their position and rights.[5] A member state wishing to extend the scope of a monopoly would have to pay compensation.

Article XII, relative to the restrictions designed to protect the balance of payments sets forth provisions similar to those of Articles XII and XVIII B of the GATT. It authorizes members whose balance of payments present serious problems (or threaten to do so) to restrict the trade in services for which they have undertaken commitments. Restrictions applied by the member must be non-discriminatory, compatible with the MFN require-ments, temporary and notified.

A member state may adopt measures that are incompatible with the agreement when its aim is to protect public morality and health (publishing or editing, for example). This exception is incorporated within the terms of Article XX of the GATT. The exceptions are important in the case of military security. They can be evoked in the case of an embargo (the United States and Nicaragua or the United States and Cuba).

The safeguard clauses are more difficult to apply with regard to services than with goods, because of the modes of delivery and the absence of detailed statistics appropriate to them, and the difficulty of distinguishing the national or foreign origin of the trade presence. In addition, the imposition of safeguard clauses may run counter to the Agreement on Trade in Services.

Commitments

Countries did not opt for the 'negative list' approach, which would have authorized countries to declare exceptions within their commitment list, but for the 'positive list' approach, which gives the countries the possibility of choosing the sector that they wish to open, as well as to specify its conditions and limits. Members liberalize sectors where they have interests or in which they wish to improve efficiency and development. Ninety-five countries offered commitment lists covering the twelve sectors mentioned above. The largest number of sectors opened concerned tourism, followed by financial services. A commitment included in a list involving services is a commitment that has been undertaken to grant access to markets and national treatment for the activities of the service in question, according to the terms and conditions indicated in the list. The government undertakes not to impose new measures restraining entry to the market or the functioning of the service. Specific commitments, therefore, have a similar effect to that of a tariff consolidation. They are a guarantee for the economic operators of other countries that the entry conditions and functioning of the market will not be changed to their detriment.

The lists of commitments agreed to by the countries are complex, since they relate to twelve sectors and 160 sub-sectors. For each sub-sector, moreover, the commitments are differentiated according to the way in which the services are provided. Countries undertake to apply basic rules for access to markets and national treatment within the selected sector. A commitment list, therefore, comprises eight headings indicating the presence or absence of limitations concerning access to markets and national treatment for each mode of supply.

Whenever the country does not mention any restriction, it undertakes to guarantee the access of foreign companies to its market or service operation. It may indicate conditions upon which access to the markets or national treatment depends for each of the four modes of providing services. When there are conditions attached to the mode of provision, the country undertakes not to apply other restrictions that would have the effect of further limiting the entry of foreign providers. But it remains free to change its regulations and possibly to revise the conditions for the entry of foreign providers by including the word 'unconsolidated' on its commitment list.

Article XXI authorizes members to modify their engagement list. Members affected by this modification may demand compensation. No proceedings, however, have yet been able to form the subject of any agreement.

Provisions for developing countries

Article IV sets out the conditions for the increased participation by developing countries through the undertaking of specific commitments. Article XII releases developing countries from their obligations when they are undergoing balance of payments difficulties. Article XIX directs countries to respect the objectives of national policy and the development level of developing countries during the forthcoming negotiations. In particular, paragraph 2 stipulates that there should be greater flexibility for these countries. The latter can require foreign providers who wish to invest in a service sector and set up a subsidiary or other form of commercial presence on their territory to fulfil certain conditions. These include the creation of co-enterprises, collaboration agreements, access for national enterprises to technologies and/or the distribution circuits and information networks of the foreign suppliers. In negotiating collaboration agreements, suppliers from developing countries may make use of the restrictions imposed by their governments in the commitment list. These restrictions are especially those that reserve authorizations to foreign service providers who agree to import the most modern technologies and train local salaried staff in their operation.

Preferential arrangements and regional integration: liberalizing services

Preferential arrangements can expedite the liberalization of services, which is sometimes more easily realized on a regional than on a multilateral basis. In 1994, eleven groups involving twenty-four countries extended their provisions to services (Prieto and Stephenson 1999: 4). Some of these have a wider covering of services than the Agreement on Services itself. NAFTA contains provisions on public procurements, whereas agreement in the WTO remains voluntary.

Within NAFTA, financial services have been liberalized. The United States and Canada have access to the Mexican financial markets, although Mexico retains restrictions on financial services (bank property, share of American and Canadian subsidiaries) and security companies (US General Accounting Office 1993: 45:7). In its liberalization process it has excluded air transport, maritime transport, telecommunications, cultural industries (film, video, recording, cable, publishing), gas, drilling and oil distribution. The APEC maintains restrictions on distribution (wholesale and retail), maritime transport and publishing.

Certain rules on origin applied by groups have the effect of increasing barriers for third countries. NAFTA is a case in point, where rules of origin in the automobile and textile fields are discriminatory (Hart 1999: 51).

Towards other negotiations

The results of the negotiations do not match the expectations of the international community, and disappointment is especially acute regarding the commitment of member states. Developed countries have committed themselves to liberalization in seventy sectors, the United States, Japan, the EU, Switzerland and Austria in more than a hundred sectors, transition countries in fifty sectors, but only 16 per cent of the developing countries have made commitments (Snape 1998: 287–288). Australia has opened eighty sectors, but one-third of its production of services was covered by liberalization commitments. A certain number of sectors remained in abeyance during the Uruguay Round and the conclusion of agreements postponed until later. These sectors were filed in the Annex to the agreement. They involve financial services, the movement of physical persons, telecommunications and maritime transport. Two sectors were not mentioned in the agreement: the activities of central banks regarding exchange rates and monetary policy, and air transport. In the latter sector, the WTO is only relevant for the maintenance, sale and marketing of computerized reservation systems.

Financial services constitute a special case. The power of the administrations that support them has enabled an avoidance of the general provisions for dispute settlement. On the other hand, safety measures adopted in the financial services sector may not conform to the agreement since their objective is to protect savers and depositors.

Negotiations on financial services commenced in April 1997 and terminated on 12 December 1997. A total of seventy members tabled their lists of concessions. The negotiations resulted in the stronger presence of foreign providers of financial services through the elimination or relaxing of limitations on foreign ownership, the institutionalization of commercial presence, and the increase in existing operations.

The negotiations on telecommunications were completed on 15 February 1997. Sixty-nine countries representing (in 1995) more than 91 per cent of the global incomes from telecommunications filed concession lists, which were annexed to the Agreement on Services. The participants – all the developed countries and six transition economies – agreed to negotiate all public and private telecommunications services relating to simultaneous transmissions in real time, including telex, fax, mobile telephone, and fixed and mobile satellite systems.

Article XIX of the agreement foresaw the continuation of the negotiations and prepared the agenda, which included the further liberalization of services, the development of rules on subsidies, safeguard measures and public procurements, and the adoption of regulations that created no barriers to trade. A special group and a regular group were established, and they are already working on the negotiations. The regular group has reviewed 600 exemptions from the MFN clause, the majority of which came from Korea, Australia and Japan.

The group is also studying air transport, where new developments have to be reviewed every five years. Since 1995, the group has adopted an overall view and examined domestic regulations, subsidies, safeguards and public procurements. It has not yet succeeded in reaching a conclusion concerning the adoption of emergency safeguard clauses, but negotiations should be completed in the not too distant future. Developing countries look favourably on this formula, which would enable them to liberalize a more substantial number of sectors, but developed countries are circumspect about the necessity of embracing such clauses.

Negotiations should involve Mode 4 in conjunction with professional services, which is of particular interest to the DCs. The right to tender professional services in all countries is subject to the possession of professional qualifications, and India and the United States have submitted a proposal that national regulations should not constitute a barrier to professional services.

The principal negotiations would have to include professional accounting, which constitutes an appreciable sector for Latin American countries desiring access to countries in the area of accounting, legal and engineering services (Croome 1998). Since 2001, numerous delegations have put forward proposals in various service areas – more than one hundred proposals presented by fifty countries covering a vast range of services. Australia has submitted proposals for maritime transport; Brazil for construction; the EU, the Dominican Republic, El Salvador and Honduras for tourism; Switzerland and the United States for audiovisual services; Canada and the MERCOSUL for computer services; and Australia, New Zealand and the United States for education.

The developing countries attach great importance to the movement of people and would welcome additional commitments. They would also like the scope of Article IV on the increased participation of the DCs to be clarified. They suffer from anti-competitive practices in the services trade.

Another important agreement is the Agreement on Intellectual Property Rights, discussed in Chapter 6.

6   The Agreement on Intellectual Property Rights

The Agreement on Trade-Related Intellectual Property Rights (TRIPS) forms the most complete multilateral agreement concluded up to the present. The TRIPS harmonizes the duration and conditions for the protection of intellectual rights and secures for WTO members the means of enforcing this protection. The agreement incorporates various conventions relative to the protection of intellectual property such as the Paris Convention for the Protection of Industrial Property[1] (1967), the Berne Convention for the Protection of Literary and Artistic Works[2] (1971), the Rome Convention on the Protection of Performing Artists, Producers of Sound Records and Broadcasting Organizations (1961) (see Box 6.1) and the 'Treaty on Intellectual Property in Respect of Integrated Circuits' (1989). The commitments deriving from these conventions are integrated in the TRIPS and have become obligations of the agreement (Articles 2:1 and 9:1).

Box 6.1 The conventions

Paris Convention for the Protection of Industrial Property (1883)

The Paris Convention was concluded in 1883 and revised several times. On 12 February 1998, 145 states were members of the convention, which was administered by the World Intellectual Property Organization (WIPO). The convention applies to invention patents, utility models, industrial designs, trademarks, service marks, trade names and indications or labels of origin, as well as to the repression of unfair trading. It extends not only to industry and trade, but also to agricultural and extractive industries, and to all manufactured or natural products.

---

continued

The contracting states are required to register intellectual property and to protect titles to intellectual property from all unfair competition.

National treatment

The convention applies the principle of 'national treatment' according to which every contracting party grants the same advantages to the foreign nationals of another contracting party as it does to its own.

Right of priority

The convention establishes a right of priority according to which it authorizes a national who has filed a patent or any other document in a member country, to protect it in any other country for a limited period of time (twelve months for a patent or utility model and six months for an industrial model and trademark).

The Paris Convention does not have any ruling on trademarks, but proposes a guide to action. A state, for example, cannot protect a trademark that is a reproduction of a trademark registered in another country. Contracting parties are not compelled to accept all the decisions taken in one of the other contracting states.

Berne Convention for the Protection of Literary and Artistic Works (1886)

The object of the convention was to protect the rights of authors in their literary and artistic works, which were previously only protected by the law of the country. It was the authors themselves who had the idea of a minimum protection extending beyond the national jurisdiction.

The convention enumerates the works and areas of literary and artistic production (music, painting, applied arts, etc.).

Principles

The convention applied three main principles:

*   National treatment (principle of international law according to which the foreigner is assimilated to the national irrespective of whether the author can request on his own territory).

- Automatic functioning of protection (abandoning formalities).
- Independence of protection.

To these principles, the convention adds some others that are of advantage to authors and editors.

First publication

Work published in a non-member country of the convention shall be published simultaneously in 130 member countries within 30 days following its publication.

Designation of domicile

An author coming from a country other than a member country of the convention but domiciled in one of the member countries shall be accorded the same protections as a national of a member country. His/her work will be protected.

Moral right

Once created, a work becomes the extension of the author as a person and confers upon it a moral right that permits the author, in addition to his/her economic rights, to oppose a distortion of the work that would prejudice his/her honour.

Economic rights

The economic value of a work is measurable and produces income for the author. There exist a whole bundle of economic rights conferred by the convention that have been retranscribed into national legislations: reproduction rights, translation rights, executory rights, and those of radio broadcasting and adaptation.

Protection

The convention protects authors who are nationals of one of the member countries, those who, while not being nationals of a member country, are publishing for the first time in one of these countries or

continued

simultaneously in a foreign country and member country, and authors who normally reside in one of the member countries.

The convention also protects those eligible persons on whom the state confers rights that go beyond the life of an author to a period of fifty years, or to fifty years from the time that a work became legally accessible to the public.

Copyrights cover all productions in the literary, scientific or artistic fields, whatever the mode or form of expression. Works that have not been fixed on a material support are attributed a separate status. The convention accords states the possibility of giving a ruling on political or legal addresses, as well as on conferences and speeches.

The convention sets forth the rights of authors over their works. It envisages, in the case where a non-member state fails to give adequate protection to the work of an author of a member state, that he/she can undertake retaliatory measures. Every forged work may be confiscated.

The convention provides for the creation of an assembly composed of convention members and an executive committee. The administrative tasks of the convention are undertaken by the WIPO.

The Rome Convention (1961)

The Rome Convention complements the Paris Convention in protecting the works of performing artists, phonogram producers and radio broadcasting organizers.

Universalizing the standards of protection

The United States and the developed countries were the forerunners of this agreement that figured among the new topics for the Uruguay Round. Their aim was to universalize their protection standards. Protection allowed them to avail themselves of the advantages of pharmaceutical, agricultural, industrial and biotechnological inventions. Research and development (R&D) of pharmaceutical products accounts for about 18 per cent of total sales and about US$500 million are required to invent a new drug, which then takes some twelve to fifteen years to reach the market (Maskus 2000: 35–36). Only six developed countries account for 70 per cent of the intellectual property rights in this domain (ibid.). However, companies are not particularly active in this domain.

Maskus emphasizes that certain industries, such as the pharmaceutical, and record and computer companies, approved of the inclusion of services in the Uruguay Round. The United States denounced the weakness of the protection accorded to property rights and urged the USTR (US Trade Representative) to act under the cover of Section 301 (Maskus 2000. http://www.iie.com). In 1986, when intellectual property forced itself onto the international agenda, an Intellectual Property Committee composed of ten to a dozen multinationals in the pharmaceutical, electronic and communications field exerted pressure on the United States President. Lobby groups as important as the Association of Pharmaceutical Producers, the Motion Picture Association of America, the Audio-Visual Industry, the Semiconductor Industry, the Californian Chemical Industry, and the Californian Wine Industry acted together within the American administration and at the international level, by mobilizing similar associations or governments in order to promote their ideas (Landau 1996).

The lack of protection of intellectual property rights in developing countries (see Figure 6.1) leads to the manufacture of counterfeits, incorrect use of trademarks, exclusion of patents for the pharmaceutical and chemical industries, and the absence of patents for biotechnological inventions. Developed countries contend that the protection of international property rights would stimulate the flow of investment into developing countries. No study, however, has justified the confirmation of such a correlation (Correa 2000: 25–29), and Primo Braga (1996), for example, notes that decisions to invest vary from sector to sector. Patents are more important in the pharmaceutical and chemical sectors than in the others, but shortcomings in protection systems have not impeded the inflow of foreign investments, and Asian countries whose legislations do not provide any protection have, in fact, been the main recipients of these.

The United States is still the uncontested leader in the field of advanced technology, but other competitors, such as Korea, Taiwan, Singapore and

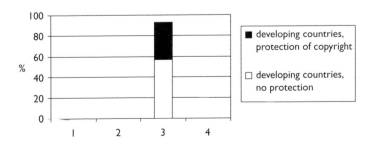

Figure 6.1 Protection of copyright in developing countries.

Brazil, are gaining ground. Subsequent to the 1970s, the share of the United States and the EC in high technology has been decreasing whereas that of Japan has doubled, advancing from 7 per cent in 1970–1973 to about 21 per cent in 1988–1989 (D'Andrea Tyson 1992: 19). Some measures adopted by the GATT in the area of intellectual property would enable protection to be enhanced in developing countries. The United States used various strategies to persuade developing countries to improve their protection system. During the 1980s, it attempted bilateral negotiations with Taiwan, Singapore, South Korea and Hungary in order that they should align themselves with the American positions, but eventually realized that they would get better results by regularizing intellectual property within a multilateral context.

Led by India and Brazil, developing countries were at first opposed to negotiations on intellectual property. They considered an agreement to be an act of technological protectionism – the northern countries generate technological innovations that are then marketed in the southern countries (Correa 2000). Developing countries form a negligible part of R&D expenses, and their share has declined from 6 per cent in 1980 to 4 per cent in 1990 despite the increase by the NIC (Newly Industrialized Countries), Korea and Taiwan. Whereas between 1977 and 1996, 95 per cent of the 650,800 licences coming from the United States were intended for developed countries, only 2 per cent of them were destined for developing countries. They cast doubt on the competence of the GATT in the sphere of intellectual property. According to them, the World Intellectual Property Organization (WIPO) was the appropriate body to deal with this. But for developed countries this organization contained no mechanism for settling differences, whereas this had emerged strengthened from the Uruguay Round negotiations.

But the developing countries were to change their mind. Mexico, Turkey and several other NICs were among the first to do this and to subscribe to the inclusion of intellectual property in the negotiation packages. The reason for this lay in the internal structuring of the Uruguay Round negotiations. The fact that various negotiations were interlinked gave the developing countries the possibility of bargaining, so that the gains were divided among the various branches of the negotiation. Bargaining between the issues was possible, and, by giving ground on intellectual property, developing countries were able to optimize their gains in other issues, such as textiles or tariff ceilings.

Negotiations, in fact, very soon went beyond these North–South cleavages to be replaced by marked divisions between the developed countries them-selves: between the United States and the EC and between the United States and Japan. This discord between the major powers gave the developing countries room for manoeuvre that they would not have had in the case of strong North–South polarization.

The conclusion of the TRIPS fulfilled a need primarily to face up to the rapid advances in technology since the setting up of the various conventions. Their field of application did not embrace the new technologies such as computer software or databases, and numerous controversies divided the countries about the best way to protect them. In Australia, for example, it was not until 1984 that the Supreme Court decided that software was a literary work and protected as such by the Berne Convention.

The TRIPS sought to fill the gaps in the conventions by extending them to the new technologies. Article 10 of the TRIPS makes it clear that computer programs and compilations of data are to be protected as literary works under the 1971 Berne Convention. The TRIPS also added location to the pre-existing rights, which applies to computer programs, cinemato-graphic works and sound recordings. It authorized the holders of copyright to prevent the hiring or sale of copies (of cassettes or computer programs) without collecting a fee.

The TRIPS established a mechanism for settling disputes, whereas the Conventions made no provision for ensuring the application of the laws whose scope and area of application had nevertheless been largely formu-lated. Many countries were dominated by pirated brands and counterfeits in spite of the national laws that prohibited them. The TRIPS mechanism for settling multilateral disputes henceforth applied to the conventions incorporated within it, together with their provisions. The agreement covers copyrights and rights relating to copyright, trademarks, geographical indication, industrial designs, patents, integrated circuit (topographical) layout designs, protection of undisclosed information and the control of anti-competitive practices in contractual licences.

Provisions of the agreement

According to the preamble, the agreement aims:

> to reduce distortions and impediments to international trade, and taking into account the need to promote effective and adequate protection of international intellectual property rights, and to ensure that measures and procedures to enforce intellectual property rights, do not themselves become barriers to legitimate trade.

Article VII specifies:

> the protection and enforcement of intellectual property rights should contribute to the promotion of technological innovation and to the

transfer and dissemination of technology, to the mutual advantage of producers and users of technological knowledge and in a manner conducive to social and economic welfare, and to a balance of rights and obligations.

The agreement sets out the minimum protection standards allowed for each category of rights. The standards relate to the protected category, the rights to be accorded and the minimum duration of the protection. In the application of these standards, the agreement stipulates that the commitments under the WIPO, the Paris and Berne Conventions must be applied to them and that members shall conform to the latest versions. The TRIPS adds a number of important commitments in areas that were not covered by these conventions.

In the sphere of copyrights, protection was granted for fifty years. Copyrights are exclusive and include the rights of reproduction, interpretation, recording, cinematography, radio broadcasting, translation and adaptation. These are not simply economic rights but also moral rights, for the holder possesses a right of control over his/her work even after cession of the economic rights. The rights are also conceded to the intermediaries who often distribute the works to the general public, such as performing artists, producers and radio broadcasting organizations. The agreement comes under the auspices of the Berne Convention, which reinforces the control and application of the agreement. It clarifies its provisions by granting protection that is no longer calculated on the basis of the author's lifetime. The innovative feature of the agreement is its extension to computer programmes and compilations of data.

The American pharmaceutical industry has strived for the enhancement of patent protection and has been the principal beneficiary (Smith 1995). Patents are protected for a period of twenty years from the filing of the patent application (Article 33). Intellectual property rights revert to the inventors and grant them exclusive property rights. Manufacturers have to procure a licence in order to be able to exploit a patent. Patents concern products and processes. They must be granted without discrimination as regards the place of invention. The TRIPS lays down the prescribed conditions for the mandatory patent licences (Article 31). Generally speaking, the country in which the patent is filed can grant a mandatory licence for the use of a patented technology if the interested user, which may be the government itself, a company or private person, has tried unsuccessfully to obtain the holder's authorization on reasonable commercial grounds.

In the case of a national emergency or other high priority situation, or in the case of public utilization for non-commercial purposes, it may dispense with this requirement. The patent holder must, however, be informed.

In the mid-1990s, certain developing countries such as Brazil, India and South Africa called for drugs used in the struggle against AIDS, the anti-retrovirals, to be made available to them at the production price rather than having to pay high prices[3] They wished to assume the right to manufacture generics.[4] Certain companies did indeed lower their selling price for developing countries, but thirty-nine pharmaceutical companies, including GlaxoSmithKline & Co, Merck, and Boehringer Ingelheim, who held patents for drugs used in the struggle against AIDS, started legal proceedings against South Africa for manufacturing drugs that it was selling to Ghana (*Wall Street Journal*, 24 April 2001).

Some of the international organizations, such as the World Health Organization and the United Nations Commission on Human Rights mobilized in support of the developing countries, and in April 2001, the pharmaceutical companies abandoned the legal proceedings against the South African government, which thus acquired the right to manufacture substitute generic drugs and also for remedies in the public procurements (WTO, 19 April 2001).

The TRIPS completed the Paris Convention provisions on the definition of a trademark, the exclusive rights of the holders of the trademark, the subordination of use to certain conditions, the licensing and cession and striking-off of a trademark. The agreement states that any sign or combination of signs that permits a product or service to be distinguished is a trademark and may be registered as such. Trademarks are accorded protection for seven years counting from the initial registration and from each renewal (Article 18).

The agreement specifies the conditions for striking off a trademark 'after an uninterrupted term of non-use of at least three years', taking into consideration the specific situation of the country. Industrial designs are protected for a minimum of ten years (Article 26:3) and the integrated circuit layout designs for ten years counting from the date of filing the application for registration or from the first exploitation if registration is not required (Article 38:2). The reinforcement of these rights should guarantee the developing countries better security for their consumer products and entrepreneurial development. Table 6.1 sets out the main terms of protection in the TRIPS.

The EC and Switzerland, by reason of their wine production, were interested in labels of origin. They did their utmost to obtain stricter rules on labels of origin, which have become semi-generic, as with champagne, for example. With regard to the United States, they were very reluctant to extend protection to this category. The TRIPS defines the geographical location. Article 22 specifies that a geographical indication seeks to inform the consumer that a product has 'a given quality, reputation or other

Table 6.1 Term of protection for categories of rights and agreements in TRIPS

Category	Term	Characteristics	Conventions and agreements
Copyrights	50 years	Observe the Berne Convention Programmes protected as literary work Protection of compilation of data Protection of rights for producers and interpreters	Berne Convention Rome Convention Geneva Convention Brussels Convention
Patents	20 years	Import right Industrial designs Applies to bio-technology and plants	Paris Convention Patent Cooperation Treaty Budapest Treaty Strasbourg Agreement
Industrial designs	7 years	Confirms and clarifies the Paris Convention Enhances the protection of known trademarks Clarifies non-utilization Geographical indications	Paris Convention Hague Agreement Nice Agreement
Integrated circuits	10 years	Protection extended to articles incorporating non-respected designs	

characteristic', that may be 'essentially attributable to its geographical origin'.

The agreement indicates that countries must not authorize the registration of trademarks containing misleading information as to the geographical origin of goods. The best-known example is that of champagne, a word associated with wine produced in a region of France. In principle, another member country is not authorized to call a wine 'champagne' when it is produced elsewhere, in Argentina or the United States for example, even if this wine can perhaps be considered comparable to French champagne in the producing country. Article XXIII grants particular protection to wines and spirits by limiting the use of geographical indications as a type or category. Nevertheless, the terms that were used in a permanent way or in good faith before 15 April 1994 may continue to be used. Negotiations should be undertaken to list the labels and arrive at a multilateral agreement

The agreement incorporates the provision of the 'Treaty on Intellectual Property in Respect of Integrated Circuits', adopted in Washington in May 1989. Articles XXXV and XXXVI require countries to protect integrated circuit layout designs. The importing or sale of articles incorporating a layout design without the authorization of the holder of the right is illegal, except for persons who were unaware of it. The latter are required to pay the holder of the right a reasonable fee while having the option to continue using the product. The agreement embodies the provisions of the Washington Treaty of 1989, which made the protection of integrated circuits universal.

Article XXXIX of the TRIPS requires protection for undisclosed information that secures an advantage for its possessor (trade secrets and know-how). Countries protect information in different ways: under legal property (United States); under the law of contract (Switzerland); or under business practice (Germany). Developing countries were opposed to considering information as part of intellectual property rights, on the grounds that disclosure was associated with the bargaining that is inseparable from intellectual property right.

The agreement does not require undisclosed information to be treated as a form of property, but decrees that a person may prevent information legally under his/her control from being disclosed to third parties or acquired or utilized by them without his/her consent and in a way that is contrary to fair trading practices. The agreement is also made up of provisions directed towards trial data and other undisclosed data that the public authorities make 'conditional upon approval for the marketing of pharmaceutical or chemical products for agriculture', and that governments of member states must protect against unfair commercial use.

Respecting intellectual property rights

The TRIPS has equipped itself with the means for ensuring respect for intellectual property rights. These means address holders of rights, customs authorities and initiators of counterfeits. The procedures that members apply must, however, prevent creating barriers to legitimate trade and offer safeguards against abusive use. They must also be fair and equitable. Decisions are to be in writing and motivated.

The agreement allows for procedures and corrective, civil and administrative measures. The national tribunals are empowered to take rapid and effective measures to prevent any introduction to trade networks and all distribution of imported goods. They may order compensation for prejudice caused. The customs authorities may prevent the circulation of goods which are thought to be counterfeit or pirated. Finally, contravention imposes penal charges. The Memorandum of Agreement on settling disputes applies to the consultations and settling of disputes under the TRIPS.

The fundamental principle of transparency applies to the TRIPS, especially that concerning notification. The laws, regulation and judicial and administrative decisions relative to intellectual property rights must be published and made available to the public in such a way that governments and holders of rights can be aware of them. Every member state is under obligation to provide information to any other member state who makes the request in writing. But no provision can compel a member to reveal confidential information.

The agreement envisaged transition periods to permit countries to align their legislation and regulations: developed countries had a year (i.e. until 1 January 1996), developing countries and transition economies five years (i.e. until 1 January 2000), and less advanced countries eleven years (i.e. until 1 January 2006).

Developed countries were also committed to offering technical and financial cooperation to developing countries and less advanced countries for the purpose of developing laws and regulations relative to the protection and respect for intellectual property rights, as well as to prevent misuse and give support concerning the establishment or reinforcement of national offices and agencies appointed to manage this protection, including staff training.

The TRIPS and developing countries

The TRIPS lays down high standards of protection. It issues directives requiring countries to introduce legislation and regulations that are harmonized as regards the protection of intellectual property rights, and which involve financial costs for developing countries. UNCTAD has calculated that these costs would amount to US$1 million. over five years for Tanzania and US$5 million for Bangladesh. The developing countries will have to extend protection to pharmaceutical and chemical products, which were excluded from their national laws. In 1994, among the ninety-eight developing member countries of the WTO, twenty-five had not yet assigned patents for chemical products, and had granted protection that was shorter than the twenty years required by the agreement. In the area of software protection, fifty-seven developing countries had not yet adopted any protection.

Nevertheless, the harmonization of protection regimes can have beneficial effects in reducing transaction costs. Differences in intellectual property regimes between countries generate effects that are similar to those of non-tariff barriers. In order to reduce the financial costs incurred in developing legislation and setting up institutions, a pooling of resources could be envisaged at this level, especially for human resources, in order to rationalize the process. Such examples of cooperation already exist between Peru and Brazil.

Protection of intellectual property rights has non-negligible commercial and financial implications for developing countries. Foreign enterprises avoid investing in countries where intellectual property is unprotected. Companies, especially pharmaceutical and chemical companies invest more willingly in countries that protect intellectual rights.

Developing countries that respect the terms of the agreement will find it easier to start up co-enterprises capable of investing more in research and development. The application of patents in these countries can encourage technically qualified persons to undertake more research and develop products that are different from those already patented. As Primo Braga (1996: 356) contends, developing countries must transform their intellectual property regimes into valid instruments for promoting innovation – a considerable challenge given the financial and institutional constraints they have to face. Technical assistance from developed countries can play a significant role at this level (*Wall Street Journal*, 19 April 2001).

The real impact of this lack of protection on the implanting of enterprises, however, is difficult to estimate. It is certainly not negligible, but it varies according to the industrial sector. Chemical and pharmaceutical industries are particularly sensitive in this respect. It must also be stressed that although the protection regimes may influence the flows of investment, these depend above all on the general political and economic climate of the country.

Those countries with knowledge are hesitant about transferring it to countries that have weak regimes due to the risks of pirating. The analyses are not conclusive, however. Conflicts arise above all in the fields of chemicals, pharmaceuticals and software, where imitation is possible independent of the transfer of technology. The decision depends more on the absorption capacity of the recipient country.

Developing countries will have interests to defend during the negotiations taking place on biotechnology and software, neither of which requires a large infrastructure. The TRIPS requires a patent to be obtained for every product or process invented in all technological domains, on condition that it is novel, and involves a new inventive activity and is suitable for an industrial application.

Article XXVII 3 (b) of the TRIPS allows for exceptions to the possibility of patenting inventions and authorizes members not to patent essentially biological processes, such as those of plants and animals, except for non-biological and micro-biological processes. Nearly thirty-one developing countries have not granted protection to their plant varieties, and few of them (except for Argentina, Kenya, Korea, Uruguay and Zimbabwe) protect their generic varieties. The TRIPS included a provision stipulating that this clause should be revised four years after the implementation of the agreement, i.e. in 1999. The question of access to genetic plant resources and the protection rights concerned were to be addressed at that time. Notwithstanding, therefore, the fact that they had a transition period available to them, developing countries, particularly those in Africa with an agricultural specialization, would have to take action and define their position in order not to miss the opportunities made available to them by this revision.

Developing countries also possess assets that can be exploited, not by using the exceptions contained in the TRIPS, but by taking advantage of certain provisions, particularly in the province of geographical indications. There are controversies, for example, concerning the provenance of 'Basmati rice'. Does it come from India, Thailand or Pakistan, or is it a generic term? It is certain that, if these three countries had protected rice in the same way as champagne and Gruyère cheese, they would have had proof of ownership at their disposal. Developing countries have everything to gain by developing small patents or utility models.[5]

The protection of patents and trademarks is undoubtedly a costly process, but developing countries have every interest in protecting their rights. Mauritanian women, by way of an example, decorate manufactured textiles that are subsequently sold in the United States, but do not receive the recompense that is due to them. Craft and traditional folk products must therefore be protected, because their creators are not remunerated and others profit from their work.

The TRIPS is a progressive agreement. A good number of issues have not yet been settled. Certain countries are not convinced of its efficiency. The TRIPS, moreover, has some implications that go beyond the agreement, such as the use of the regulations relative to competition, the possibility that the imposition of patents on pharmaceutical and biotechnological products should not cause price rises, and the effect of intellectual property rights on the environment (Maskus 2000b: 137).

7   Measures concerning trade-related investment

The first attempts to develop regional and multilateral rules concerning foreign investment date back to the Havana Charter of 1947. From the end of the 1940s, various instruments were devised that reflected the priorities of the time. Chronologically, the period extending from the 1950s to 1970s was especially preoccupied with controlling foreign investments. Developing countries sought to retain their national sovereignty, and foreign investors sought to protect their investments against political risks and the nationalisation of their assets. In this respect, Decision 24, adopted by the Andean Pact, symbolized these concerns.

At the same time, at the multilateral level, negotiations started under the umbrella of the United Nations regarding a code of conduct for multilateral enterprises, but this has never been applied. In 1980, the UNCTAD developed a body of principles and rules on restrictive trade practices that was accepted by the member states, but lacked a binding force. Bilateral agreements covered the treatment and the legal protection of foreign investors following their entry and establishment in the host countries. The question that remains concerns the effect that these agreements have had on the flow of investments. The North American Free Trade Agreement (NAFTA) was innovative in the investment area. It applied national treatment for 'the establishment, acquisition, expansion, management, conduct, operation, sales and other provisions concerning investments', but specified exceptions and set up a mechanism for settling disputes.

The United States militated in favour of including an agreement on investments in the negotiations, and called for an integrated and coherent approach that was in line with the changes in the trading system. Services and investments were subject to retaliatory measures under Section 301.[1] Developing countries, however, considered that the American efforts were aimed at legitimizing the application of trade barriers against their exported goods in the case of restrictions on foreign investment. They therefore demanded that investments should only be treated according to their trade-related aspects, and stressed that certain measures relating to investment or content of nationally produced products were essential for channelling foreign investments in conformity with their development aims. These measures were used to counter the anti-competitive practices of the transnationals.

The Agreement on Trade-related Investment Measures (TRIMS)

The area of application of the Agreement on Trade-related Investment Measures (TRIMS) is relatively limited. The WTO Agreement makes no ruling on the admission of foreign investment or on the inducements that governments offered to attract foreign investment (financial inducements, tax reductions and the granting of land and various services under preferential conditions), or even upon possible exclusions or restrictions existing at the national level. On the other hand, certain conditions relative to the structure of property and nature of the operations (percentage of local labour employed, products of national origin, employment of a certain percentage of local inputs in production) imposed by the countries fall within the area of application of the TRIMS Agreement. The Agreement on Services also contains provisions that apply to investment, particularly in respect of trade presence.[2] Developing countries associate provisions on investment with the movement of persons (Mayasheki and Gibbs 1999: 6).

The agreement applies to the provisions of the General Agreement on Trade including Article XI on the prohibition of the restrictions on imports and Article III on national treatment, which come into force when investors undertake the purchase of a certain percentage of local products – the measure of 'local content'. Article III applies in this case, since there may be discrimination between imported and national products.

Nowadays, a certain number of developing countries impose rules on the content of national products in order to direct the allocation of resources towards sectors in which they are interested or in order to attract investment. The majority of these countries, however, are reviewing the maintenance of such measures within the context of the open trading policies that they have now adopted and the measures they are taking to attract foreign investment. Thus the agreement only serves to emphasize an already existing tendency towards the elimination of trade-related investment measures, which are held to be incompatible with GATT. The agreement provides a list of these measures:

- prescribing that an enterprise shall sell or employ products of national origin or coming from a completely national source, whether specifically relating to certain products determined by volume or value of the product, or by a proportion of the volume or value of its local production;

- requiring the purchase or use by an enterprise of imported products limited to an amount related to the volume or value of the local products that it exports;
- requiring the elimination of quantitative restrictions (Article XI.1 of the GATT) on the import or export of products by an enterprise;
- import by an enterprise of products used or connected with its local production, in a general way, or by limiting it to an amount allied to the volume or value of the local production that it exports;
- import by an enterprise of products employed or related to its local production, by limiting the access of the enterprise to currency by an amount conditional upon the entry of currency attributable to the enterprise;
- export or sale for export of products, whether specifically relating to particular products, a particular volume or value of products or a proportion of the volume or value of its local production.

The area of application of the agreement is limited. It only defines investment measures held to be incompatible with GATT and arranges a transition period for countries to eliminate them. It does not, for example, prevent countries from resorting to other measures, such as making investment conditional upon export results. It does not prohibit them, moreover, from requiring that a certain percentage of the equity capital must be held by local investors, or that a foreign investor must introduce the most recent technology or carry out a certain level or type of R&D locally.

The agreement envisages a transition period for eliminating prohibited TRIMS of two years for developed countries, five for developing countries and seven years for transition countries following the operative date of the agreement. In addition, the agreement reaffirms the commitments to transparency and notification that are effective for all the other agreements. Article 5.3 of the agreement gives the Goods Council the possibility of prolonging the transition period for developing countries. These may also perhaps require more flexibility when the transition period ends.

Article 9 of the agreement contains the possibility of future work in five years time on competition and investment. The mandate of the working party on trade and investment set up after the Singapore Conference in 1996 did not specifically relate to these negotiations, but aimed at facilitating exchanges of view between the members on the political, economic and legal aspects of trade and investment.

A certain number of countries, including those in development, support the idea of a multilateral approach for direct foreign investments. The existence of 1,500 bilateral agreements on the promotion and protection of investments, and regional and multilateral agreements – some of which we shall discuss later – argue for a unified and multilateral approach to investments. There is room for negotiation, for most of the bilateral agreements concern investments already existing in the territory of a country but have little to say about the admission of new foreign investments.

These bilateral agreements leave complete freedom for countries to determine the conditions under which they admit foreign investment. It is possible that developed countries tend to limit the flexibility in the framework of a multilateral agreement and to impose more restrictive conditions. Any simplification that would tend to reduce the debate on investments to a North–South issue would be dangerous, but divisions do exist within the developed countries. Japan, Canada and the EU support the idea of a negotiation within the WTO, but the United States is reticent about this. There are developing countries, particularly in Latin America, that support the idea of a multilateral approach to investments, but others, namely from Asia, are more sceptical.

Certain countries insist that the negotiations should include problems of international trade linked to the restrictive trade practices and anti-competitive behaviour of transnational companies. Negotiations on investment are connected to other agreements. Establishing a commercial presence in a country through the inflow of foreign investments is essential for the services domain, and services, therefore, create the conditions for a liberalization of investment.

Another major agreement is that on textiles and clothing, and this is discussed in Chapter 8.

8 The Agreement on Textiles and Clothing

Non-discrimination was one of the basic principles of the GATT. It prohibited the use of quantitative restrictions but permitted them insofar as they were not discriminatory. Nevertheless, many countries have applied quantitative restrictions subsequent to the GATT by invoking the provisions relative to balance of payments problems. This provision was used by the textile sector, particularly in developed countries (essentially North America and Europe), to protect themselves against textile exports from developing countries. The textile trade was to be subject to different rules from those applied to other goods. The textile trade (beginning with cotton) was exempted from the GATT rules on protective measures. Forced to do so by President Kennedy, importing and exporting countries signed a multilateral agreement, entitled the Short-Term Arrangement, concerning the international textile trade. This arrangement authorized countries to protect their textile industries by imposing quantitative restrictions.

The GATT did not condemn this arrangement. A working party that met in order to examine the problems of the textile sector authorized import restrictions in cases of prejudice to a particular sector (*market disruption*) arising from a specific country.

In 1972, negotiations started under the auspices of GATT and concluded with the Multifibre Arrangement (MFA), which became effective in 1974, for a period of four years (1974–1977). Fifty countries signed it, including China. It was of a transitory nature, renegotiated in 1977 and then replaced by MFA II (1977–1981), MFA III (1981–1986) and finally by MFA IV, which was to expire in 1991 but did not do so until 31 December 1994. The list of textile products included in the MFA, which never ceased to lengthen, included natural, synthetic and artificial fibres. It was an 'umbrella agreement' – governments, including the USA, the EU and Canada, were able to adopt restrictive measures and negotiate bilateral agreements with developing countries (South-East Asia, Brazil, India and Pakistan). These agreements numbered more than one hundred. MFA IV was more restrictive than the previous arrangements since it covered a greater number of products. The measures adopted aimed at reducing imports by additional quotas on fibres, wool and manufactured fibres, and by imposing compensatory rights and rules of origin in order to avoid transhipment.

When the Uruguay Round negotiations began, almost 60 per cent of the world trade in textiles and clothing was subject to the MFA (35 per cent for clothing and 43 per cent for textiles).[1] Developing countries were the most affected, among them India, Pakistan, Bangladesh and Indonesia, even though their total exports of textiles and clothing accounted for 45 per cent of global exports.

In spite of the MFA, the textile trade became five times more important and that of clothing eleven times more important than in 1974. This increase was an expression of the desire of the countries to increase the added value of the products they exported. The clothing sector exceeded that of textiles and represented a market of US$158,000 million. The number of producers was limited, and in 1993 ten countries accounted for 62 per cent of world trade, including six developed countries, three newly industrialized countries and China.

A transition agreement

The Agreement on Textiles and Clothing (ATC) organizes the transition from the multifibre arrangement to the normal WTO regime, and is scheduled to disappear at the end of the transition period arranged for 1 January 2005. At that date the Multifibre Arrangement will end, together with the quota system under its aegis. The textile and clothing trade will then be subject to GATT discipline. Apart from the particular quantitative restrictions on a given product by a given country, the other standards that apply to the textile trade are those of the 1994 GATT, and WTO members will have to comply with them. Developing countries are accorded a special and differentiated treatment that is specific to the ATC.

The Multifibre Arrangement is situated outside the GATT regulations, whereas the ATC is an integral part of the WTO. The preamble to the agreement specifies that its aim is to 'permit the eventual integration of this sector into GATT on the basis of strengthened GATT rules and disciplines, thereby also contributing to the objective of further liberalization of trade'.

At the end of the transition period (1995–2005), the quantitative restrictions will be eliminated. In consequence, any possible restrictions will be in the form of tariffs according to the GATT regime. The agreement cannot be extended. Article 9 states that: 'This Agreement and all restrictions thereunder shall stand terminated on the first day of the 121st month that the

WTO Agreement is in effect, on which date the textiles and clothing sector shall be fully integrated into GATT 1994.'

The programme ensures that the area of application of the agreement and the volume of trade shall develop in such a way as to liberalize the sector by integrating the products in the general regime by liberalizing the quotas inherited from the ATC and progressively eliminating the quantitative restrictions that do not conform to the general regime. The restrictions cannot be repealed in a day. The agreement stipulates that: '*The process would have to be of a progressive nature*'.

During the transition period, a member state may impose restrictions on imports if it can prove that the growth in imports is seriously harming its production. It may resort to a transition safeguarding mechanism.

Four successive stages

The agreement comprised four successive stages. The first commenced in 1994 and ended in 1997. The second stage covered a period of four years until 2001, and the third three years. The last stage finishes on 31 December 2004. The agreement lists the products covered in an Annex and envisages their integration into the general system. As this integration took place, the quantitative restrictions inherited from the Multifibre Arrangement had to be liberalized. All WTO members were able to adopt specific safeguard measures on condition that they notified them. A large number of provisions related to these notifications. The agreement also contains a supervisory Textile Monitoring Body (TMB).

At each stage in the integration, members must give quite early notification of products, differing according to the countries that they wish to exclude from ATC application. As soon as they are notified, these products are no longer subject to ATC rules, but only to those of the WTO. If these integrated products had been affected by a quota by way of the ATC, this disappears immediately. The country in question may no longer invoke Article 6 in order to protect the industry producing these products.

At each stage, the products integrated by a WTO member must comprise at least one product from among the following: combed and spun, fabrics, ready-made articles and clothes. During the first stage, 16 per cent of the products covering this group were integrated.[2] On 1 January 1998, 17 per cent of the products were added. On 1 January 2002, 18 per cent were integrated, bringing the number up to 55 per cent, and on 1 January 2005, it will be 49 per cent.

At the beginning of the integration process, two types of situation relative to the integration process were possible. Members who imposed restrictions by way of the MFA of 31 December 1994 (Canada, the EU, the USA and

Norway) had to undertake the integration process in its entirety. They could either retain the possibility of using the ATC safeguard measures, in which case they had to prepare and notify an integration programme, or not use this possibility, in which case they had to integrate their textile and clothing products within the 1994 GATT and were exempted from the integration programme. Members who resorted to quantitative restrictions were required to notify the WTO about the products concerned, levels of quotas, annual growth and possible flexibility rate, before 31 December 1994. These quotas, negotiated within the framework of bilateral agreements could not be modified, but were subject to a process of liberalization.

Coefficients of growth applicable to the quotas inherited from the MFA through Article 2.1 were no longer quotas fixed by virtue of bilateral agreements, and could not be changed even by common accord between the parties. In order to improve and widen access to textile products, the agreement envisaged accelerated increase in growth coefficients arranged for the annual review of quotas fixed for each category of textile products by virtue of bilateral agreements.

Third World countries could undertake counter-notifications in order to inform the WTO of possible restrictions concerning textile and clothing products that were maintained by the MFA.[3] In this case, members would have a year in which to eliminate them or to present a programme of progressive suppression.

Balance of the first and second stages

The agreement did not specify the allocation of the products to be integrated within the different categories (combed and spun, fabrics, ready-made articles and clothing). When the agreement reached the first stage in 1995, combed and spun represented 70 per cent of the integrated products. Clothes represented only a small proportion.

According to Article 2, 'each Member shall integrate into GATT 1994 products which accounted for not less than 16 per cent of the total volume of the Member's 1990 imports of the products in the Annex'. The Article did not indicate that the member must liberalize 16 per cent of the products subject to quantitative restrictions, but simply that the products must represent 16 per cent of the total 1990 imports. Products of low added-value were the first textile products to be integrated, and those that were more sensitive were left until later. In the first series of integration measures taken on 1 January 1995, neither the USA nor the EU included textile and clothing products that were subject to quantitative restrictions. Including products not subject to restrictions served only to swell the volume of imports for integration, and in order to reach the objectives set by the agreement in terms of volume, the USA and the EU integrated products high in volume but low in value.

At the end of the second stage, 17 per cent more were integrated, bringing the total up to 33 per cent. The result confirmed the first tendencies in terms of the market access of products subject to quantitative restrictions, although one of the important consequences was the irreversible integration of the selected products. Certain products figuring in the lists of products selected by the USA and the EU were subject to quotas. The importing of T-shirts, trousers and shirts was still very limited in the USA, and that of cotton fabrics in the EU. The products selected by the USA as objects of restrictions, such as children's clothes, coats and hosiery, formed a small proportion of such products (Pinnell 2001). Norway eliminated a certain number of quotas by way of Article 2.15 of the agreement, and by the end of 1998, it had in fact abolished almost all its quotas with the exception of fishing nets from Indonesia, Thailand and Malaysia. Canada did likewise.

After 1 January 2005, no country will be able to maintain restrictions on the import of textiles unless it can justify this by way of the safeguard provisions of the agreement, and these involve an enquiry and demonstration that the increase in imports is seriously harming its textile industry. These restrictions would, moreover, have to be applied independently of the source of the products, as with the restriction instituted by the MFA.

During the transition period, Article 6 authorizes countries to resort provisionally to a safeguard mechanism on non-integrated textile products if the sudden increase in imports threatens the sector or is seriously damaging the national production of similar or directly competitive products, on condition that this can be substantiated. The use of the Article 6 clauses is not open to all members. They must either have maintained some quantitative restrictions within the framework of the MFA (the EU, the USA, Norway and Canada), or have notified it. The safeguard mechanism comprises two stages. First, the country proposes applying the safeguard measure and recognizes that the situation justifies resort to such a measure. Second, it indicates the countries whose exports are harming the production sector.

The agreement specifies a number of precise and constraining parameters that the member state must follow in order to apply the safeguard mechanism. It must consult the selected country and allow sixty days in order to convince the country that the situation is such as to justify the restriction. If the country is not convinced and there is no agreement between the parties, the member state has thirty days in which to decide whether or not to impose a measure that will come into operation within ninety days at the latest following the consultation request. The measure must fulfil certain criteria, including that the minimum level of the quota depends on the former trade over the first twelve and last fourteen months.

A quota may not last for more than three years and cannot be extended. The member state must start the procedure contained in Article again 6 if it has not introduced a measure within a time limit of ninety days, or if it wishes to continue protecting its industry after a period of three years. This quota must be accompanied by a growth coefficient of at least 6 per cent per year. It is for this reason to some extent negotiable, except in the case of wool products imported into the USA, where they introduced this particular clause at the time of concluding the agreement.[4]

In the case of the MFA and the bilateral agreements, the coefficients of growth were often less than 6 per cent, which was, nevertheless, the norm within the arrangement. The measure is reviewed by the TMB, which has to declare its admissibility within thirty days. Up to the present, the monitoring body has not declared any measure to be in conformity with the agreement. The decision has been followed in effect in all cases. Unlike the mechanism for settling disputes, members have a moral but non-absolute obligation to follow the rulings of the TMB. If a member state decides not to follow them, it has thirty days in which to inform the WTO. The TMB examines these reasons during the thirty days and may modify its recommendations or maintain them. The country may appeal to the normal WTO settlement mechanism. The process that took place within the scope of the ATC replaces the first stage of the regulation process.

Member countries realize that the provisions of the agreement in no way permit a return to the MFA. The member state must justify its action and show that the imports from a country have suddenly increased and are threatening its sector. It may in fact happen in effect that there has been an increase from this country but imports from other countries have decreased. In such a case, the safeguard measure cannot be applied.

The USA has had considerable recourse to provisional safeguard methods – twenty-four during the first year of the agreement. Two cases were submitted for dispute settlement. The litigants, India and Costa Rica, won the case. The decisions of the TMB and the Dispute Settlement Body have clarified how the agreement has to be applied. Subsequently, the USA has only applied the safeguard measures five times.

On the other hand, certain countries, such as Brazil and Colombia, which were victims of the MFA, have also used Article 6. In these two cases, the TMB decided that they had to discontinue the measures adopted. The EU has employed anti-dumping measures for products that were already subject to quantitative restrictions.

Multilateral surveillance is applied at two levels. At the technical and legal level, it is ensured by the Textiles Monitoring Body and, at the political level, by the members within the Council on Trade in Goods. Supervision of the implementation of the agreement is the responsibility of the TMB

(Article 8). Unlike the other WTO bodies, this consists of a president and ten members nominated in their personal capacity. It was modelled partly on an institution that existed in the MFA, and partly on the idea that a small number of members facilitate quick decisions. The member seats on the TMB are allocated to informal groups from WTO members whose composition was chosen by the WTO members. These informal groups select the countries that are to nominate a member to sit on the TMB. Provisions are taken in order to attribute the seats by rotation. Members do not attempt to give instructions to the TMB members nor to influence them. The TMB meets every month and decision is by consensus.

The Council on Trade in Goods also surveys the agreement at a more political level, and discusses the report that is submitted to it every year by the TMB. A year before the end of each stage, the Council reviews the implementation of the agreement in depth and examines the functioning of the system on the basis of a report provided by the TMB (in 1997, 2001 and 2003).

Special provisions for developing countries

The special provisions concerning developing countries are contained essentially in Articles 1 and 6 of the agreement, and envisage a special and more favourable treatment for certain categories of suppliers and certain types of trade.

Least-developed country members

- The third paragraph of the preamble recalls 'that it was agreed that special treatment should be accorded to the least-developed country members'.
- A note at the bottom of the page relative to Article 1.2 specifies that, as far as possible, exports to least-developed country members should also benefit from the provisions of Article 2.18 (improved access for small suppliers) and of Article 6.6 (accorded differential and more favourable treatment in the fixing of the economic terms agreed in application of Article 6). For this reason, almost every least-developed country has benefited from the application of the provisions of Article 2.18.
- Article 6.6 urges that, in applying the transition safeguard mechanism, least-developed country members should be granted a markedly more favourable treatment, preferably in all its elements but at least overall, than that accorded to the other groups that are mentioned in this paragraph. Since no member has notified the application of a safeguard measure regarding imports from a least-developed country member, these provisions have not been applied.

Small suppliers and newcomers to the market

These least-developed country members must benefit as much as possible from the conditions envisaged by Article 2.18 and 6.6. Members involved (Canada, the EU and the USA) have applied the provisions of Article 2.18 using different methodologies, but all have chosen to apply growth coefficients with a stage in advance.

Cotton-producing and cotton-exporting members

Article 1.4 stipulates, 'the particular interests of the cotton-producing exporting Members should, in consultation with them, be reflected in the implementation of the provisions of this Agreement'. Members have different conceptions of the way in which the particular interests of cotton-producing and cotton-exporting members should be – and have been – envisaged in implementing the ATC provisions. Cotton-producing and cotton-exporting members are indeed of the opinion that since no consultations were initiated by the importing countries, these provisions have not been applied. Importing members have declared that they have been faithfully applied.

Wool-producing and wool-exporting members

Article 6.6 stipulates in paragraph (c) that:

> with respect to wool products from wool-producing developing country Members whose economy and textiles and clothing trade are dependent on the wool sector, whose total textile and clothing exports consist almost exclusively of wool products, and whose volume of textiles and clothing trade is comparatively small in the markets of the importing Members, special consideration shall be given to the export needs of such Members when considering quota levels, growth rates and flexibility.

This provision has never had to be applied.

Re-imports

Article 6.6 (d) states that:

> more favourable treatment shall be accorded to re-imports by a Member of textile and clothing products that Member has exported to another

Member for processing and subsequent reimportation, as defined by the laws and practices of the importing Member, and subject to satisfactory control and certification procedures, when these products are imported from a Member for which this type of trade represents a significant proportion of its total exports of textiles and clothing.

Generally speaking, the USA has envisaged a more favourable treatment for this type of trade. Nevertheless, the report of a special group examining the restriction imposed by this member concerning certain imports from Costa Rica decided that the USA had violated their obligations under Article 6.6 (d).

Special treatment of members who were not MFA members

Article 1.3 stipulates that:

> Members shall have due regard to the situation of those Members which have not accepted the Protocols extending the Arrangement Regarding International Trade in Textiles since 1986 and, to the extent possible, shall afford them special treatment in applying the provisions of this Agreement.

The TMB has not received any information concerning the frequency of recourse to this provision. It should be noted, however, that no measure has been adopted as regards imports by non-MFA members.

Notification commitments

Concerning notification commitments, the deadlines have increased for certain groups of countries.

Textiles and rules of origin

Certain factors that do not come within the ambit of the WTO Agreements have, nevertheless a major influence on the way that business circles view the WTO Agreements and their application. Rules of origin come within this category (see Box 8.1).

Box 8.1   Cumulation of origins in community agreements

According to the principle of the cumulation of origins, it is possible for an African country to import textile components and export them as originating from the Africa Caribbean Pacific (ACP) zone, which is not acceptable according to the agreement. A product enters freely into the EU provided that it comes from the ACP zone. The system authorizes the cumulation of origins, i.e. that the product may contain components from outside the regional area on condition that it is part of a coherent geographical entity. Plurality is authorized for the countries of Central America (Columbia, Costa Rica, Salvador, Guatemala, Honduras, Nicaragua, Panama and Venezuela), and for Algeria, Morocco and Tunisia in Africa. The plurality threshold has been extended under the Lomé IV Agreement from 10 to 15 per cent.

The rules of origin are stricter for textile products. For certain countries they constituted a real barrier to trade in manufactured goods in that they exclude simple assembly within the country receiving the preference, fix ceilings for foreign materials at 40 or 50 per cent, and require textile or clothing products to originate from the fibre.

According to the Generalized System of Preferences (GSP), 'the rule of double transformation' predominates. If the thread is imported by a country that weaves it, the product is considered as originating from that country. If the fabric is manufactured in one country and exported to another, where it is transformed, the final product exported to the EC loses its privilege.

Box 8.2   Rules of origin applied by NAFTA

The North American Free Trade Agreement (NAFTA) determines the origin, not according to the last 'substantial change' in the product – i.e. the process that transformed it into a new article – but when it follows a tariff change. A product qualifies for NAFTA and is imported without customs duty into the USA, Canada or Mexico, if it has been produced, manufactured or cut in one of the member countries, or if it has undergone a change in the tariff classification. For certain products, moreover, the original NAFTA value must reach a certain percentage of the total value of the product, the 'regional

---

value content'. As for textiles, the rule of origin rests on the principle of 'thread first' (cotton, synthetic fibres, spun fibres and sewing thread), i.e. to profit from all the advantages, the textiles and articles of clothing must be manufactured on the basis of thread produced in a NAFTA member state. There are some authorized exceptions for filament threads from outside the NAFTA. The thread principle prevails for fabric and articles of clothing, except for certain articles such as bags, curtains, and silk and linen goods. Substrates of petro-chemical origin for thread may come from outside NAFTA.

The Agreement on Textiles and Clothing and Africa

Generally speaking, the Sub-Saharan countries that were not signatories to the Agreement on Textiles and Clothing (ATC) are affected very little by it, insofar as they export little to the 'traditional' importers (the EU, the USA, etc.), and do not use the ATC to protect themselves. The sector may, however, be important for certain countries, of which South Africa is an example. In 1995, its textile exports rose to US$160 million. Other countries are also exporters, although to a lesser degree: Côte d'Ivoire (US$33 million, jeans exported to the USA), Zambia (US$34 million), Zimbabwe (US$32 million), Nigeria (US$18 million), Cameroon (US$11 million) and Mauritius. The USA grants trade preferences to African textile-exporting countries. Tunisia was not an MFA signatory, but it has concluded preferential agreement with the EU. Textiles are the primary export sector in Tunisia, provide added value and employ 250,000 people.

The African Growth and Opportunity Act (AGOA) was agreed in 2000 and aimed to help transform the political landscape of Sub-Saharan Africa, stimulating the textile exports of the region. Substantially all products for Sub-Saharan Africa are now eligible to enter the United States duty free. The United States imported US$8.2 billion of duty free goods in 2001 under AGOA, representing almost 40 per cent of all US imports from Sub-Saharan Africa. The United States is Sub-Saharan Africa's largest single market, purchasing 27 per cent of the region's exports in 2000.

AGOA's trade and investment-centred policy is also reinforcing Africa's own economic and political reform efforts; providing greater African access to US technical assistance and trade finance facilities; and promoting high level US–Sub-Saharan Africa dialogue on trade and investment issues. Thirty-five Sub-Saharan African countries have been designated as AGOA beneficiaries. Over 1,800 additional products from Sub-Saharan Africa were designated for duty-free access to the United States, in addition to the 4,650 products already eligible under GSP. As of April 2002, seventeen Sub-Saharan African countries had been designated for AGOA apparel benefits, with six others in the process of meeting the requirements.

9 The WTO and regional integration

Compatible or contradictory?

The GATT is based on one fundamental principle: non-discrimination. The Most Favoured Nation clause commits members to extend trade advantages contracted with one member to all other members. Free trade areas, customs unions and preferential agreements contravene this rule, in that they grant concessions to member countries that are not necessarily extended to third countries. Regional arrangements are based therefore on discrimination.

Nevertheless, the founding fathers of the GATT recognized that, in certain cases, regional integration constituted a step towards realizing the liberalization of trade, one of the principal objectives of the GATT, and therefore exempted it from the Most Favoured Nation clause. The contracting parties had to give a ruling on the compatibility of the regional agreement with the GATT provisions, and prepare periodic reports on the application of the agreement clauses according to the transition phases. But during the examination of the Treaty of Rome, the contracting parties were unable to reach agreement on the compatibility of the Treaty of Rome with the GATT, and the European Union, for its part, did not wish the contracting parties to adopt a decision. Since then, the legal status of the regional agreements has remained very vague and, with the exception of a single case,[1] it has been impossible to decide on the compatibility between the regional arrangements and the provisions of the GATT.

In view of the extent and proliferation of the regional agreements,[2] the phenomenon raises a fundamental question. Does regional integration promote free trade or is it contrary to this liberal regime? Recent studies have shown that regional integration complements the multilateral trading system rather than opposing it. Regional integration constitutes a laboratory in which to test measures for the liberalization of trade. According to Fred Bergsten, 'regional integration and the easing of trade restrictions can help to keep the machine turning over' (1996: 7).

Article XXIV and the Memorandum of Agreement on the interpretation of Article XXIV of the General Agreement on Tariffs and Trade of 1994, the enabling clause of Article V of the Agreement on Services,[3] remain the principal provisions for the free trade areas, customs unions and provisional agreements. Although the Memorandum of Agreement on the interpretation of Article XXIV clarifies certain aspects of the Article that were the most controversial, it still does not resolve all aspects. Before considering Article XXIV and the Memorandum of Agreement, we shall briefly examine the enabling clause. The second part of the chapter will be devoted more specifically to the effects and limits of regional integration.

Provisions of the GATT and the WTO: Article XXIX

Article XXIV aims at to clarify the conditions under which a regional arrangement, free trade area, customs union or interim arrangement that, after a transition period, may give rise to a customs union or free trade area that is compatible with the GATT. According to this Article, any preferential agreement between developed countries or between the latter and developing countries containing tariff preferences on a defined number of sectors is, on principle, compatible with the WTO. These arrangements must satisfy Article 4 of Article XXIV, in that they have been created in order to facilitate trade and not to form new trade barriers against non-member countries. The important paragraphs of Article XXIV are numbers 4, 5, 6, 7 and 8. The others have a more limited scope.

Article XXIV aims at ensuring that a regional arrangement results in creating trade and not in diverting it, and that the adverse effects of trade are reduced to the minimum. It stipulates that customs duties and restrictive trade rules must be eliminated substantially on all sectors of trade originating from the territories of the regional area (Article XXIV 8 (b)).

Concerning the main principles of the WTO, Article XXIV pursues three objectives:

- transparency
- coherence
- tariff negotiation.

Transparency and coherence

Article XXIV 7 (a) requires members who have decided to enter a customs union, to become part of a free trade area or to participate in a provisional agreement, to inform the contracting parties *without delay* and to provide all information. The members shall examine the agreement and communicate their reports and recommendations. The contracting parties had decided in

1971 that the regional arrangements should submit a report to the Council every two years. These reports were in fact communicated until 1987, when this activity was interrupted. All notifications will be examined by a working party.

The expression 'without delay' has given rise to different interpretations. Should it imply after application or before ratification?[4] Although it is true that the majority of the regional arrangements did fulfil these requirements and notified the WTO just as they had for the GATT, some considerable delays were discernible between the signature of the regional agreements and the notification, because most member countries preferred to notify once the agreement had been ratified. According to Article 4, the objective for establishing a customs union or free trade area must be to facilitate trade between the constituent territories and not to hinder the trade of other WTO members with these territories.

The agreement defines the customs union as the substitution of a single customs area for two or more areas, when the effect of this substitution is that customs duties and other regulatory trade restrictions are substantially eliminated from the trade relations between the constituent territories, and that the customs duties and regulations applied to territories that are not included in this are identical (Article 8 (a) (i) and (ii)).

A free trade area is a group of two or more customs areas between which customs duties and other restrictive trade regulations are substantially eliminated from trade concerning products originating from the constituent territories of the free trade area (Article 8 (b)). According to Article 5 (b), the customs duties and other trade regulations affecting the trade of group members with non-members must not be substantially higher or more rigorous than were the duties and regulations prior to the setting up of the free trade area or conclusion of the provisional agreement.

According to Article 5 (c), a provisional agreement comprises a plan and programme for the establishment, within a reasonable period of time, of the customs union or free trade area.

Memorandum of Agreement on the interpretation of Article XXIV

Examination of the GATT regional arrangements has raised many problems. Certain provisions of Article XXIV, especially Articles 4 and 5, were unclear and subject to divergent interpretations. In addition, the number of regional arrangements has multiplied over recent decades, and this has necessitated a re-examination. Their nature has changed, moreover, and the cover of the arrangement exceeds the simple trade provisions.

The Singapore ministerial declaration stresses that:

The trade relations of the WTO Members are increasingly subject to the influence of regional trade agreements, whose number, extent and area have considerably increased. These initiatives may encourage a greater liberalization and assist the least advanced, developing and transition economies to integrate within the international system. . . . The expansion and extent of the regional trade agreements make it important to analyse the WTO system of rights and obligations, insofar as the relations with the regional trade agreements need to be clarified. We must still reaffirm the primacy of the multilateral trade system.

Evaluation of global incidence

Paragraph 5 (a) of Article XXIV deals with the global incidence of customs duties and other commercial regulations applicable before and after the establishment of a customs union. Customs duties and other commercial regulations must not have a higher global incidence[5] than before the establishment of the union. Evaluation shall be based on a global evaluation of the weighted rates of duties and customs duties levied.

The customs union must provide statistics on the imports during a previous representative period, which are to be communicated in value and volume to the Secretariat according to the tariff line, and apportioned according to WTO member's country of origin. The Secretariat to which the statistics have been sent calculates the average weighted duties according to an accurate method, which was employed during the Uruguay Round multilateral trade negotiations. With a view to an evaluation of the global incidence of the other trade regulations, which is difficult to quantify and aggregate, an examination of each measure, regulation, targeted product and trade flow may be necessary.

The reasonable time limit mentioned in paragraph 5 (c) of Article XXIV should not exceed ten years except in exceptional cases. In the case where ten years are insufficient, a detailed explanation would have to be presented to the Council for Trade.

Renegotiation of consolidated duty

Problems at this level lay in the time limit for the negotiation, and the form of compensation in the shape of reductions in customs duties on other tariff lines. The Memorandum of Agreement reaffirms that the procedure under Article XXVIII of the GATT must be followed before the tariff concessions are modified or withdrawn during the setting up of a customs union. Negotiations shall be undertaken in good faith with the object of achieving mutually satisfying compensations. These must take into consideration the reductions in customs duties on the same tariff line. In the case where these negotiations are unsuccessful, the customs union is free to modify or withdraw the concessions. But the members concerned are equally free to withdraw those that are substantially equivalent.

Article XXIV 7 (a) requires members who decide to enter a customs union, join a free trade area or participate in a provisional agreement to inform the contracting parties without delay and provide them with all the necessary information. Members shall examine the agreement and submit their reports and recommendations to the Council for Trade in Goods. In 1971, the contracting parties had decided that the regional arrangements should submit a report to the Council every two years. The problems at the examination level lay in the lack of recommendations, the agenda and the reports being too widely spaced.

The memorandum specifies that all notifications shall be examined by a working party, which will submit a report to the Council for the Trade in Goods. The latter can make such recommendations to the members that it considers appropriate. Concerning the provisional agreements, the working party may make suitable recommendations about the proposed calendar and the necessary measures for the definitive employment of the customs union or free trade area. If necessary, it can order a new examination of the agreement.

All substantial changes in the plan and programme incorporated within this agreement must be notified to the Council for the Trade in Goods. In the case where a notified provisional agreement does not include such a plan and programme, the parties shall not maintain, or shall abstain from enforcing the agreement, if they are not ready to make the recommended changes. A later examination of the implementation of these recommendations shall be envisaged.

Dispute settlements

The memorandum endeavours to correct the lack of settled conclusions that characterized the previous system. Only one regional arrangement had been declared incompatible with the GATT. The provisions relating to the dispute settlements may be invoked for all questions arising from the application of the provisions of Article XXIV relative to customs unions, free trade areas and provisional agreements.

Article XXIV 4 lays down that the aim of a regional arrangement must be to facilitate trade between the other parties and the constituting territories. Is this a general principle that must guide the criteria according to which a customs union of free trade area shall be compatible with the GATT, and in accordance with paragraph 5, according to which the provisions of the agreement must not form a barrier to the establishment of a customs union and a free trade area? Is this an additional requirement that would be added to the other provisions? If that were indeed the case, it would be necessary to resolve the question according to which the members of a customs union should not raise barriers to a particular contracting party. But this interpretation would be in contradiction to Article XXIV 5 and 6.

There is no agreement on the range of the 'other trade regulations' under Article XXIV 5, which limits the examination to tariffs. Does this phrase cover quantitative restrictions or rules of origin in the case of free trade areas, which are sometimes complex and restrictive? The interpretation of the term 'substantially all sectors of trade', used in Article XXIV 8 is subject to controversy. For those who are of the opinion that the term 'substantially' implies a percentage, what is the percentage of trade? The present tendency is to situate 'substantially' at 90 per cent. Others estimate that this 'substantially' does not relate to a percentage but qualitatively, because certain arrangements exclude a whole sector from trade liberalization, especially agriculture. The agreements concluded by the EC and its peripheries bear witness to this selectivity.

These agreements aim at a liberalization of trade in industrial products but are only partially open to farming products. The only reference offered by the Memorandum of Understanding on the interpretation of Article XXIV is to be found in the preamble, according to which

> [the] 'contribution to the expansion of world trade that may be made by closer integration between the economies of the parties to such agreements . . . is increased if the elimination of duties and other restrictive regulations of commerce extends to all trade, and diminished if any major sector of trade is excluded.

The sentence: 'customs duties and other regulations applied by each of the members of the union with territories that are not included in it shall be substantially identical', that is used in Article XXIV 8 (a) (ii) has also caused controversy. The question is whether the other commercial regulations include quantitative restrictions, and whether, in consequence, the members of the customs union must use common quotas. Does the expression: 'restrictive commercial restrictions' used in Article XXIV (b) include duties of a taxation nature and tax expenses, and rules of origin concerning the free trade areas and provisional agreements? Article XXIV does not mention Article XIX in the list of restrictive commercial restrictions that it has drawn up. This omission raises a question that is both legal and economic. Is the list indicative and exhaustive? There are some who assert that it is economically impossible to maintain safeguarding measures when the aim of a free trade area or customs union is to improve the competitiveness of the industries of the member countries.

The enabling clause applies to the arrangement between developing countries. It specifies differentiated and more favourable treatment, reciprocity and fuller participation by developing countries, and recognizes the role of regional integration in augmenting freedom of trade through closer integration between the economies of member states.

This decision, adopted at the conclusion of the Tokyo Round negotiations (1973–1979), grants developing countries a differentiated and more favourable treatment on the MFN basis. Paragraph 2 (c) of the clause applies this treatment to the regional and global arrangements, the aim of which is the mutual reduction or elimination of customs duties or non-tariff measures. The WTO has imposed a strict discipline on transparency. Member countries must notify the agreements, submit all necessary information and start consultations.

Examination procedures of the regional arrangements

As we have seen above, Article XXIV 7 (a) requires members who decide to enter a customs union, join a free trade area or participate in a provisional agreement, to immediately inform the contracting parties and provide all the necessary information. The members shall examine the agreement and submit their reports and recommendations to the Council of Trade in Goods.

In 1966, the members of the WTO decided to set up a Committee for Regional Arrangements to examine, among other things, the regional arrangements notified to the WTO. The Committee would carry out a systematic analysis of the regional arrangements. This analysis was necessary because the regional agreements had proliferated, and also in certain cases overlapped. The Committee will examine the arrangements and prepare a report. Until now, the examination process has been carried out on the basis of questions and answers – a procedure similar to that employed for admission to the WTO. The Committee will also have to agree on the terms of reference and examine ways of improving and facilitating the examination. Such procedures would, however, involve rather long time periods and introduce considerable delays between the submission time of the report and the setting up of the regional agreement. This could have some negative effects on the recommendations that were possibly contained in the report.

The Committee of Trade and Development is responsible for the notifications it receives under cover of the enabling clause. It must decide upon the terms of reference and make possible recommendations. The Committee of Trade in Services fulfils the same functions, but is covered by Article V of the Agreement on Services

Regional integration: advantages and limits

Regional integration includes very different experiences, which range from a preferential arrangement to a free trade area or a customs union. A free trade area aims at eliminating trade barriers between member countries of the area, who nevertheless maintain their commercial policy with respect to third countries. In a customs union, the member countries do not eliminate customs duties between themselves, but also adopt a common external tariff. The third stage involves setting up a common market and harmonizing the macro-economic policies.

In recent decades, regional integration has become increasingly important. Following the first wave of regional arrangements in the 1960s, there was a second wave in the 1990s. New arrangements have emerged, others have been transformed. The Caribbean Common Market, the Central American Common Market (CACM) and MERCOSUR are examples of regional integrations that have grown stronger over recent years.

In Africa, the West African Economic and Monetary Union (UEMOA), which aims at establishing a common market and monetary area, the Common Market for East and Central Africa (COMESA), and the South African Development Community (SADC) have adopted new strategies to strengthen their regional ties. In West Africa, the UEMOA, which replaced the Economic and Monetary Union of West Africa (CEDEAO), was created in January 1994. It includes francophone and anglophone countries.

In 1990, the CEDEAO reactivated the original treaty and set about a vast trade liberalization programme in industrial goods that was to be completed in 2005. The first ten years were devoted to removing tariff and non-tariff barriers and developing a common external tariff. The liberalization is graduated according to the categories, which take account of development levels. Thus the Côte d'Ivoire, Ghana, Nigeria and Senegal should have finished the liberalization process within six years, whereas Burkina Faso, Cape Verde, Gambia, Guinea-Bissau, Mali, Mauritania and Niger were to finish in ten.

In Central Africa, the Central African Economic and Monetary Community (CEMAC), comprising Cameroon, the Central African Republic, Chad, Congo-Brazzaville, Equatorial Guinea and Gabon replaced the UDEAC. The group is oriented towards a common market by combining the elements of a customs union and economic and commercial integration pursued by the UDEAC.

In South Africa, several groups overlap. At the widest level, the Common Market for South and East Africa (COMESA) aims at creating a customs union followed by a unified common market. A tariff reduction programme, developed in 1987, envisaged a gradual reduction of customs duties, to be completed by 2000. Created in November 1993, it succeeded the Preferential Trade Zone for South and East Africa. As for the SADC, this succeeded the SADCC. It included the South African Customs Union (SACU), which grouped South Africa, Botswana, Swaziland, Lesotho and Namibia. It comprises fourteen members and foresees the setting up of a free trade area within eight years. The participation of South Africa and Mauritius, with their thriving economies, guarantees the SADC certain advantages.

The benefits of regional integration

It is not our intention to present an exhaustive list of the advantages of regional integration, but just to cite a few of them. Regional integration increases the size of the market, thus enabling economies of scale, which will help reduce production costs. It rationalizes the industrial fabric through the closing down of low-production units and transferring them to more dynamic areas. These elements are especially useful for small and medium-sized economies. Regional integration reinforces the competitiveness of the member states by reducing production distortions.

According to some, regional integration constitutes a transition step towards global integration, since the production structure is not oriented towards the sub-regional market. Within the UEMOA, Burkina Faso or Benin are 60 to 70 per cent dependent on cotton. Export markets are no longer situated in the developed countries. Real growth has returned towards developing countries, especially South Asia and Latin America.

Commitment to greater freedom in world trade will of necessity have an impact on the preferences enjoyed by developing countries. These have for a long time obtained concessions that enabled them to compete with better-endowed countries. The General System of Preferences (GSP), or the advantages obtained by the Lomé Agreement, do not play a major part in the export structure of the Africa Caribbean Pacific (ACP) countries. The share of community imports of manufactured and non-manufactured products from the ACP has not stopped falling since the creation of the Lomé Agreement, declining from 6.7 per cent in 1976 to 3.1 per cent in 1993.

It is the least-advanced countries that will be most eroded by the GSP, i.e. the forty-eight countries, of which thirty-nine belong to the ACP. Table 9.1 shows the particular situation of these countries relative to the main players (the EU, the USA and Japan). The erosion of the preferences is most clear-cut in the case of tropical products imported by the EU countries. The loss

Table 9.1 Preferential margins and loss of margins (%)

	Preferential margin			ACP (Africa)	GSP (Africa)
	Before the Uruguay Round	After the Uruguay Round	Loss of margin	Loss of margin	Loss of margin
The EU					
All products GSP	8.42	5.7	2.72	3.91	3.35
Non-tropical agriculture	6.02	1.89	4.13	13.01	5.2
Tropical agriculture	4.27	1.11	3.61	4.72	2.93
Japan					
All products GSP	6.73	2.61	4.12	3.23	
Non-tropical agriculture	15.77	5.59	10.18	5.83	
Tropical agriculture	21.18	7.23	13.59	3.86	
The USA					
All products GSP	4.87	2.44	2.43	1.66	
Non-tropical agriculture	7.41	5.04	2.37	0.52	
Tropical agriculture	7.17	4.71	2.46	3.79	

Sources: UNCTAD (1994b), Organization of African Unity (1994).

for these products, as well as for the farming products, is estimated at from 29 per cent to 45 per cent respectively. The loss for products destined for Japan is about 63 per cent.

The rules of origin are very important. Chapter 10 discusses the Agreement on the Rules of Origin.

10 The Agreement on Rules of Origin

As defined by the Agreement on the Rules of Origin, the rules of origin are the laws, regulations and the administrative decisions for general application that enable the establishment of a country of origin for merchandise. In a globalized world, however, given the many changes and numerous components coming from various countries, they are increasingly difficult to establish. Producers divide up the production process into many geographically localized stages, and it is difficult to trace the exact origin of a product. The production process is divided between a pre-assembly and assembly phase and is carried out on a global basis (Landau 2001: 122). The *maquiladora* in Mexico, who undertake assembly operations for American companies, accounted in 1994 for US$23,000 million – almost half the Mexican exports to the USA (World Bank 1997: 43). Most of the present-day products are manufactured in more than one country. More than 80 per cent of the semi-conductors destined for the American markets are assembled and tested abroad, mainly in the five South-east Asian countries (D'Andrea Tyson 1992).

Computer enterprises in the USA share production between specialized producers. Enterprises in Thailand and China assemble the circuits, the program is written in Bangalore in India, Malaysia and the Philippines assemble the components, and Taiwan and Korea specialize in the high added-value services and memory (Steinberg 1998: 25). Manufacturing of automobiles in the United States involves nine countries for the production, marketing and distribution, of which 30 per cent is found in Korea for assembly operations, 17.5 per cent in Japan, 7.5 per cent in Germany, for design, 2.5 per cent in Taiwan, for publicity and marketing activities, and 1.5 per cent in Ireland and Barbados, for the data. Only 37 per cent of the production is generated within the USA.

International sourcing for intermediate inputs has increased more rapidly than the supply from domestic sources. Yeats has estimated that the production division accounts for US$800,000 million, or nearly 3 per cent of the world trade in manufactured products (WTO 1999). This shows the growing interdependence of countries. The sharing of the production is of very great importance to developing countries. They import components and parts and re-export them to their places of origin.

The success of South Asia has is due to this rapid accumulation of capital, and from the apprenticeship process and growth of productivity accompanied by an increase in wages (UNCTAD 1998). The wage increases have reduced the advantages that these countries derived from such industries as textiles and clothing, which constituted the export industries during an initial phase of their development, and one of the responses has been a relocalization of the industries to other countries of the region, such as Malaysia, Thailand and China. The second response has been a turning towards industries with a high concentration of capital and technology, such as electronics, machinery and transport equipment. In nine years, 80,000 Taiwan enterprises have thus moved, half of them to China and the other half to East Asia (*The Economist*, 24 March 1998).

The imposition of anti-dumping or compensatory duties and the administration of quotas in the textile domain are based on the origin of the product. Rules of origin are also employed for branding 'manufactured in', as well as for the attribution of public procurements and the compilation of trade statistics. They are also important in the case of preferential trade agreements. In these cases, the rules of origin determine the advantage or not of preferences and reduced customs duties.

Rules of origin are very varied. Certain countries even apply different rules of origin according to their trade policy instrument. No precise provision concerning rules of origin was provided in the GATT 1947. Each member state was free to decide its own rules. Changes affecting the world economy since the 1980s have helped to draw attention to the problems raised by the existence of different rules of origin, and have encouraged research into the harmonization of them.

Aim of the agreement

The Agreement on the Rules of Origin fills a gap. Only the International Kyoto Agreement on the simplification and harmonization of customs procedures (1973) provided the guidelines for establishing the origin of a product, but these recommendations were not compulsory.

The aim of the agreement is to establish and apply, in a transparent way, rules of origin that are clear, predictable and coherent, and assist the flow of trade. For this, the agreement aims at a harmonization of the non-preferential rules of origin. Even though the harmonization is limited to the non-preferential rules, however, the agreement introduces a common declaration in the Annex, which also relates to preferential rules

Disciplines

The agreement imposes disciplines, based generally on the principles of transparency, that are applicable during and after the transition period. A country may not modify its rules of origin without previously publishing them, and may not apply them retroactively. It must give the member states the opportunity of resorting to the tribunals or independent judicial, arbitral or administrative procedures, as well as protecting confidential information.

The agreement also includes an original clause. Any person having valid grounds may request the customs authorities of a member country for appreciations on the origin that they would attribute to a given merchandise. These appreciations of origin shall be provided as early as possible, but within 150 days at the latest and shall generally remain operative for three years. The same provision will apply in the case of preferential rules of origin.

Rules of origin must not in themselves be used as instruments of commercial policy, impose unduly rigorous restrictions, or require as a pre-condition the respect of a certain condition unconnected with the manufacture or processing.

A Committee on Rules of Origin at the WTO and a Technical Committee under the auspices of the Customs Cooperation Council (CCC) were set up. The Committee meets at least once annually, and all members are part of it. They also participate in the Technical Committee.

The harmonization process

The harmonization programme forms the most important part of the agreement. It envisages the setting up of rules of origin based on the following criteria:

- Merchandise wholly obtained in a country and minimum operations or procedures.
- Substantial transformation, involving a change in the tariff classification based on the harmonized system or SH.[1] Origin is conferred on a product if, after transformation, it is classified under a position (or sub-position) that is different from that before the transformation.
- Supplementary criteria. When the criteria below are not applicable, other criteria, such as that of an *ad valorem* percentage and/or that of the manufacturing or processing operation, are necessary for conferring the origin of the product.

The harmonization process is not simple. The work of the Technical Committee on the rules of origin were to be finished in July 1998, but were extended well beyond that date. The working party have to review the products, chapter by chapter and sub-position by sub-position. As of now, the Committee has reached an agreement on 1,730 sub-positions of the 5,130 that constitute the SH universe. Some of them are very sensitive and are of great importance, not only for developed countries, but also for those that are developing, especially for textile and agricultural products. Since they involve industries that are subject to the globalization process, such as the watch, food and textile sectors, they are all the more difficult to deal with.

The decisions of the Technical Committee are submitted to the WTO Committee on the Rules of Origin, which either approves them or returns them for further development. Products have been classified into several categories:

- products for which there is an agreement
- products for which there is no agreement
- products that have not yet been examined.

Members must notify their non-preferential rules of origin (Article 5). Ninety countries have done so up to the present. Members must also notify the Committee of the preferential rules of origin (Para. 4 of Annex II) (see Box 10.1). In the case of countries that are members of several regional agreements, the preferential rules of origin may not be uniform, depending on the specific agreement.

Box 10.1   Preferential rules of origin

The system controlling the rules of origin in the Lomé Agreement distinguished between an entirely produced and an entirely originating product. An originating product must, after the addition of inputs coming from various countries, undergo a change in its tariff line. The transformation does not need to be substantial. It can be minimal. The agreement provides a list of criteria. The system authorizes the plurality of origins, that is to say that the product may contain components from outside the regional area, on condition that they come from the Africa Caribbean Pacific (ACP) zone or form a coherent geographical entity. Plurality is authorized for the Central America countries (Colombia, Costa Rica, El Salvador, Guatemala, Honduras, Nicaragua, Panama and Venezuela), and for African countries it is authorized for Algeria, Egypt, Morocco and Tunisia.

The WTO dispute settlement mechanism applies to the rules of origin. Until now, only a single case been submitted for settlement. In July 1996, the USA introduced some changes in the rules of origin for silk accessories and silk and textile products in silk, dyed and printed cotton, and in vegetable fibres dyed and printed by hand. The USA considered that these products, labelled 'Made in France', arrived in a finished state and were only cut and mounted in Europe in order to be imported into the USA. For this reason, they could not be admitted into the USA as originating from France, but had to be taxed as textile products from India, China or another country of origin where they had undergone the most substantial processing.[2] The EU considered that the USA were contravening Article 7 of the Agreement on Rules of Origin, Article 8.4 of the Agreement on Textiles and Clothing, and Article XXII of the 1994 GATT.

11 The Agreement on Subsidies and Compensatory Measures

The USA promoted the idea of a negotiation on subsidies and compensatory rights a year before the commencement of the Uruguay Round. It was preoccupied by the question of agricultural subsidies, but its attitude was prompted by the desire to end once and for all this practice that constituted a barrier to trade. At the heart of the problem was Article XVI of the GATT, which regulated the employment of subsidies but did not forbid them. Other aspects also concerned Article VI, which covered anti-dumping and compensatory measures.

Under the Tokyo Round, a code was developed for subsidies that sought to specify the functioning and obligations of the contracting parties, as well as investigations provoked by the industries concerned. But the code sought, primarily, to reconcile divergent interests, those of the USA, for example, which condemned the use of subsidies by foreign governments (especially the EU with regard to agriculture) and the practice of compensatory rights that they themselves used.

Negotiations on subsidies were complex. They were broken down into several sections and negotiated separately. Agricultural subsidies were treated in the agricultural dossier, those on civil aviation were excluded, and those concerning coal and steel were incorporated in the dossier on natural resources. Compensatory rights were treated concurrently with subsidies. The GATT proposed listing the subsidies that were to be definitively eliminated and those that were to be subject to restrictions.

General features of the Agreement on Subsidies and Compensatory Measures

The agreement concerns two questions that are separate but closely associated: (1) multilateral disciplines that regulate the granting of subsidies; and (2) the resort to compensatory measures that are intended to neutralize the prejudice caused by the subsidized imports.

The agreement lays down two rights of appeal for a member state that considers itself to be disadvantaged. The first is multilateral and subject to the multilateral regulations that determine the granting of subsidies. The second is unilateral. Members may unilaterally adopt compensatory measures with a view to neutralizing the prejudice caused by the subsidized imports, or by appealing to the WTO mechanism for the dispute settlements. Although it is unilateral, a compensatory measure may only be adopted following an investigation, the procedure for which is carefully regulated by the agreement. The member state that has been injured must prove the existence of a link between the subsidy and the prejudice caused to a national industry. The request must be introduced by the sector of national production, or in its name if it is supported by national producers whose total sum of productions amount to more than 50 per cent of the total national production of the similar product.

The Agreement on Subsidies specifies the definition of a subsidy as: 'A subsidy is considered to exist if there is a financial contribution by a government or any public body of the local jurisdiction of a member that confers a benefit.' In this definition there are three important elements for a subsidy and they must all be present for a subsidy to exist: (1) a financial contribution; (2) an intervention by the government or public body of the local jurisdiction; and (3) a benefit.

1   *Financial contribution.* This was included in the agreement after lengthy negotiations. Certain members maintained that there could be no subsidy as long as no expenses were appropriated by the member state budget, whereas others considered that certain operations no less implied public expenditures and should be considered as subsidies.

    According to the SCM (Subsidies and Compensatory Measures) Agreement, there cannot be subsidies without expenses appropriated by the member state budget. The agreement includes a list of the types of measures that constitute a contribution. These comprise direct transfers of funds as gifts, loans or contributions to the issued capital, and indirect transfers from funds such as loan guarantees, tax incentives and provision of goods or services and purchases of goods.

2   *Measures taken by government agencies.* The agreement applies to measures taken by public authorities and lower echelons, as well as by public bodies and state-owned companies.

3   *Benefit.* The agreement remains vaguer concerning the benefit conferred, and issues partial directives. A benefit may be determined by a commercial criterion or in relation to the costs incurred by the public authorities approving the subsidy. Article 14 of the agreement states that

the existence of a benefit may be determined (but not necessarily) in relation to a commercial criterion.

A subsidy is only a subsidy if it includes these three elements. It must be granted specifically, moreover, to an enterprise or production sector, or to a group of enterprises and production centres. Only the specificity of the subsidy has a distorting effect that may be corrected. If subsidies are granted to a large number of beneficiaries within a country, they have no distorting effect.

The agreement does not aim to limit unduly the right of governments to grant subsidies, but seeks to prevent or dissuade them from employing subsidies that have an unfavourable effect on the trade of other countries.

These three categories of subsidies are designated by the colours of traffic lights. Red corresponds to prohibited subsidies, amber to subsidies that may give rise to an action, and green for those that do not.

The three categories of subsidies

- Export subsidies are prohibited. In the past, the rule forbidding the use of subsidies in order to benefit exports of industrial products was only applied to developed countries; the agreement now extends it to developing countries. The latter have a transition period at their disposal to make their subsidy practices conform to the rules. During this period, they are not permitted to increase the level of their export subsidies. The prohibition does not apply to less advanced countries (LDCs), or to DCs whose GNP per inhabitant is less than US$1,000. DCs whose exports of one or several products have become competitive must discontinue the subsidies within a period of two years. Article 27.6 sets the level of competitive exporting as being that which reaches 3.25 per cent of world trade during two successive calendar years.
- Permitted subsidies that may give rise to an action are not prohibited, but they may be contested either by the dispute settlement mechanism, or with the help of a compensatory measure if they would have unfavourable effects. The agreement classifies these effects:

    - A loss incurred by a production sector on account of the imports. The agreement authorizes the levying of a compensatory right.
    - Serious prejudice sustained by a production sector of the importing country. In this case, a right may indeed be exercised if the investigation by the authorities has established the existence of a causal link between the subsidized imports or dumping and serious prejudice sustained by the production sector concerned. An

investigation must be initiated, moreover, at the request of the production sector that considers itself harmed by the imports. DCs and those in transition are granted special treatment and a transition period of from two, seven or eight years, according to their situation, and LDCs are granted the free resort to subsidies.

- The annulment or reduction of advantages resulting from the GATT 1994 comes about most frequently when the improved market access that is supposed to result from a consolidated tariff reduction is compromised by the subsidy. In this case, the agreement permits a call for action, because there is a refutable presumption that serious prejudice exists.

• Permissible subsidies do not give rise to an action (Article 8). The agreement sets out three cases of subsidies that do not give rise to actions, either because the risks of causing distortions to trade are minor, or because they are of particular importance:

- subsidies granted by the public authorities to LDCs defined on the basis of their turnover or workforce;
- subsidies for research carried out by enterprises in order to adapt their production facilities to new environmental requirements;
- aid for disadvantaged regions, on condition that the aid is not reserved for certain enterprises or production sectors in the region.

The list of prohibited subsidies is exhaustive. That of export subsidies appearing in Annex 1 of the agreement is not but the list is illustrative. With regard to the subsidies that do not constitute grounds for an action, the list is exhaustive. All subsidies must be notified to the Subsidies and Compensatory Measures Committee (Article 25), and all notifications must be renewed every three years. These are carefully examined by the Committee.

Part V of the agreement sets out the rules to be obeyed when applying compensatory measures, as well as to carry out investigations that may lead to the application of a measure. A compensatory measure is taken unilaterally, but it may only be adopted after the member has proceeded to an investigation and when it has fulfilled the criteria set out in the agreement concerning the existence of a causal link between the subsidized imports and the prejudice sustained by the production sector. The agreement introduces an original element in that it authorizes the total effects caused by imports from several members.

Investigations

The investigation must be presented in writing by the national production sector, or in its name if it is supported by national producers whose total sum of production constitutes more than 50 per cent of the similar product. The authorities have to open the investigation if they are in possession of sufficient proof of a subsidy, prejudice, and a causal link. Investigations leading to the imposition of a compensatory measure are subject to precise rules guaranteeing their transparency. All parties involved must provide the information required from them and not hinder the progress of the investigation. They must also be able to defend their interests. The authorities must inform all the members and parties concerned of the facts examined, and they must also be able to justify their decision. Consultations have to be held throughout the investigation.

To prove the existence of prejudice, the investigation has to take account of all the factors other than the subsidized imports that cause, or are liable to cause, prejudice to the sector. Primarily, the relevant factors comprise the volume and prices of the non-subsidized imports of the product, the contraction in demand or changes in the configuration of consumption, the restrictive practices of the foreign and national producers, and the competition between these same producers, the development of techniques and the effect on the export and productivity of the national production sector.

To determine the threat of prejudice, however, the authorities have to examine, among other things, the nature and effects of the subsidies in question, the rate of growth of the subsidized imports in the internal market, and the adequate and freely available capacity of the exporter (or its imminent and substantial increase). There is also the question of imports entering at prices whose effect would be to depress internal prices or prevent them from rising appreciably, and thus probably increase the demand for new imports and stocks of the product forming the object of the investigation.

Provisional measures may not be taken before 60 days, calculated from the beginning of the investigation. These may take the form of compensatory rights guaranteed by cash deposits or guarantees equalling the amount of the provisionally estimated subsidy, but must not exceed four months.

If the authorities of the importing member have provisionally established the existence of a subsidy and of prejudice caused by it, certain commitments are possible. But resort to these is limited to those that would serve to terminate the investigations and thus avoid the application of arrangements for auto-limitation, or similar measures disguised as such.

The application of a compensatory measure is limited to five years, except where its application is justified by an extension of the prejudice. An independent tribunal must be set up in order to verify whether the investigations are compatible with the internal legislation.

Special provisions for DCs

LDCs, and DCs whose GNP per inhabitant is less than US$1,000 a year and are listed in the Annex, are completely exempt from the rule precluding export subsidies. Nevertheless, if the exports of a product become competitive, these countries are required to eliminate export subsidies for the product within a time limit of eight years, instead of the two years stipulated for other developing countries.

Other DCs have a transition period of eight years for dismantling – preferably in a progressive way – their existing subsidy arrangements. Throughout this period they may not raise the level of their subsidies or grant subsidies for products that did not previously benefit from them. Enterprises that are at present benefiting from export subsidies must therefore prepare themselves for the day when the governments will discontinue them at the end of a transition period. DCs whose GNP is less than US$1,000 per inhabitant (Bolivia, Cameroon, Côte d'Ivoire, Egypt, Ghana, Guatemala, Guyana, India, Indonesia, Kenya, Morocco, Nicaragua, Nigeria, Pakistan, Philippines, Dominican Republic, Senegal, Sri Lanka and Zimbabwe) are subject to the same provisions as those that are applicable to other DCs.

Transition economies have seven years in which to progressively remove prohibited subsidies that have previously been notified within the two years subsequent to the agreement coming into effect.

Although DCs are authorized to maintain export subsidies within the transition period, the importing countries (including DCs) can take countermeasures during this time if these are harmful to their national production sectors.

12 The WTO and developing countries

Towards an equality of power?

The Uruguay Round signalled the end of the great power supremacy of the USA, the European Union, Canada and Japan. Without underestimating their weight during the economic negotiations, the Uruguay Round marked a turning point in the relations between the developing countries (DCs) and the GATT. India, Brazil and, more generally the medium-sized powers, adopted a new approach to trade negotiations, by drawing closer to the power circle. In previous negotiations the DCs had remained on the fringe of the GATT, since their aim was then to obtain preferences from the developed countries. Few DCs participated in the essential part of the negotiations, which was concerned with the exchange of tariff concessions. During the Uruguay Round, however, they participated independently or in coalitions, and sought to consolidate discipline and multilateral rules, the only means capable of protecting them from the imbalance of power and the injustices arising from it. The preferences they obtained from the developed countries, in particular the EU, did not contribute an increase in their share of the world market.

From 1990 to 1996, exports of goods from Africa increased by only 2 per cent, whereas they represented 5 per cent of the world exports. Many factors contributed to these results. The exports were mainly dominated by raw materials, whereas the global demand for coffee, cocao and tobacco had never ceased to decline. Regional integration also contributed towards decreasing exports by favouring exports from the regional zone. Whereas 45 per cent of the clothing exports from Africa were exposed to quantitative restrictions in the developed markets, this applied to only 5 per cent of those coming from OECD countries. It remains true, however, that exports from Africa suffered less than those from other DCs.

Only 19 per cent of African textile exports were subject to quotas, as against 53 per cent in the other DCs. Finally, the Uruguay Round resulted in the erosion of generalized preferences and of those of the Lomé Agreement. An UNCTAD study has estimated that the erosion of preferences granted to the Sub-Saharan countries equals a loss of US$900 million or less than 0.3 per cent of the exports in 1992 (http://www.itd.org). This is a modest amount, and would have been far greater if the EU had reduced the advantages that it awards to DCs in the generalized preferences system.

Special and differential treatment

Until the Uruguay Round, DCs were exempt from most of the rules that applied to the developed countries. They were exempted from the tariff concessions and were able to employ the subsidies as a development tool. Their relations with the developed countries were subject to non-reciprocity and enabled them to maintain protection when they considered it necessary. They enjoyed a special and differentiated treatment. In 1954–1955, Article XVIII of GATT was amended in order to allow the DCs facing balance of payments problems to adopt quantitative restrictions on their imports. Ten years after the creation of the GATT, a committee of experts concluded that any sort of barrier contributes to the trade problems of DCs.

The GATT then set up the Haberler Committee on trading measures that could not be settled by an improved treatment for DCs. The latter reacted in 1963 by calling for an action programme against quantitative restrictions and customs duties that hit their exports of tropical products, and for the elimination of internal taxes.

In the 1960s, the GATT tried to bridge to the gap between developed and developing countries. Article XVIII 'the governmental assistance to economic development' allowed the DCs: (1) to maintain flexibility in the tariff structure to protect their infant industries; and (2) to apply quantitative restrictions on the balance of payments that would take into account their need for imports. In 1968, the DCs obtained preferences and the GATT granted them with the enabling clause, which allowed them to do the following:

- have preferential access to the developed countries' markets;
- have differential and more favourable treatment for non-tariff barriers;
- support their exports by subsidies;
- conclude regional agreements among the least-developed countries to reduce or eradicate tariffs;
- have a special and differential treatment for least-developed countries;
- obtain no reciprocity in trade relations.

The GATT then adopted some amendments in 1965, which were in response to the creation of UNCTAD in 1964. The fourth part of the GATT concerns trade and development. Articles XXXVI to XXXVIII required more favourable conditions of market access to be granted to products of interest to DCs (especially primary and manufactured products), and called for an action that was coordinated with international agreements, in order to improve this access. DCs are also exempt from the most favoured nation clause for a period of ten years. But the GATT did not contribute to an improvement in the situation of these countries. Industrialized countries continued to levy high customs duties on DC exports and the successive Rounds have only produced a very slight reduction in these. Agriculture – an important export sector – continues to be excluded from the GATT rules.

The 1979 Habilitation Clause laid down the principle of differentiated and more favourable treatment for DCs, reciprocity and full participation in GATT activities, as well as preferential market access based on non-reciprocity and non-discrimination. There was furthermore to be more favourable treatment for the rules concerning non-tariff barriers, and special treatment for the least-developed countries (LDCs). This treatment enabled the latter to remain unaffected by the codes negotiated during the Tokyo Round concerning export subsidies, technical and trade barriers and public procurements. In return, the DCs accepted the 'gradual' principle that modified the extent of their rights and obligations as they climbed the ladder of economic growth, since they would then no longer be able to justify the special and differentiated treatment hitherto accorded to them. For the DCs, the situation remained precarious, and developed countries continued to erect new non-tariff barriers that harmed their exports. The Multifibre Agreement threatened their exports of textile products and the developed countries imposed voluntary export limitations on shoes, iron, steel and non-ferrous metals. The escalation of tariffs was substantial.

From marginality to active participation

In 1982, the USA applied pressure to change the 'arena' of negotiation, which was henceforth to include agriculture, services and intellectual property, but the Group of 10[1] were opposed to supporting a new round of negotiations while many of the Tokyo Round dossiers still remained in suspense. They met regularly and maintained a common front, although certain of them recognized that pursuing an obstructionist strategy was doomed in the long run to failure. The discussions remained deadlocked until the meeting of the GATT Council in 1985, when the USA, employing an unusual strategy for that body, called for a vote to decide on a special session of the contracting parties. Two-thirds of these supported the American proposal, and the unity of developing countries disintegrated. Beside the irrepressibles, led by Brazil and India, there were moderates who, for economic or political reasons, rallied to the idea of new negotiations. The strategies of the players were no longer determined according to simple divisions and systematic polarizations, but were decided by more complex motivations and evaluations.

In January 1986, a preparatory committee was made responsible for establishing the objectives, subjects and procedures for the negotiations. Three texts were presented. The first of these originated from the G9 – a European Free Trade Association (EFTA) group, Canada, Australia and Zealand and joined by the G20 led by Colombia and Jamaica. The second was from the G10 (the resistant group), and the third from Argentina, which prepared a compromise text. The USA, Japan and the EU did not participate in this process, but were consulted by the G9. When the Punta del Este Conference opened, the 'café au lait' proposal originating from the G9 – a joint effort by Switzerland and Colombia – served as the basic text for the official opening declaration of the negotiations.

The Uruguay Round ended in a dilution of the special and differentiated treatment. The developed countries declared that they could no longer tolerate 'free riders' (beneficiaries offering no compensation in return), whereas certain developing countries were becoming increasingly integrated within the world system. In the final Act, special treatment was limited to transition periods for applying agreements and receiving technical assistance. What has been the impact of the Uruguay Round on developing countries? Has the WTO assisted their integration into the global economy?

The WTO succeeded in increasing the division between the DCs that had abandoned an import substitution strategy and adopted free trade, and those that had not succeeded in so doing. The Latin American and Asian countries had unilaterally liberalized their economy, but certain other countries, among them those from Africa, had not abandoned the Third World system of import substitution prevalent in the 1970s. This approach, advanced by Raul Prebisch and the Economic Commission for Latin America (ECLA), was seen as the most rational method for ensuring equitable development and protection of infant industries. Prebisch maintained that, from the 1950s onwards, the trade from the DCs had not ceased to diminish, whereas the industrialized countries had become ever more prosperous. From the 1960s onwards, the views held by Prebisch became those of the Third World when they were officially accepted during the first United Nations Conference on Trade and Development (UNCTAD) in 1964.

The decline in trade from the South arose through the trading policies of the Northern countries, which amassed a stock of raw materials and set up tariff and non-tariff barriers against Southern exports. Countries from the South demanded rights within the international economic system, including that of choosing the development model that was best adapted to their culture, and political system.

This strategy was also favoured by the 'Dependence' school supported by Samir Amin. It had its origins in the theory of Frederic List, according to which, countries pass through various stages of development – from pastoral to agriculture, agricultural to manufacture, and trade. The transition from one stage to another cannot come about automatically, and countries must for a certain time protect their infant industries. Industrialization by free trade is only possible if all the countries are at the same development stage, a situation that cannot be applied to DCs. These do not have an industrial base that is adequate for competition with industrialized countries by giving free rein to the situation. Protection of infant industries is therefore necessary in order to stimulate the productive power of countries that lack an adequate industrial base (Shafaedin 2000). The strategy of import substitution combines various instruments: tariffs and import bans, accompanied by a system of restricting the circulation of capital. Tariffs must increase when production commences, thus giving the government the budgetary means for planning economic development. But the use of quantitative restrictions and exchange controls encourages a fixed income attitude. Import substitution increases the vulnerability of DCs to external shocks and rural poverty (Krueger 1988).

This strategy had important consequences in terms of diplomacy. In the 1970s, DCs were more interested in the UNCTAD than in the GATT, which was dedicated to the market economy principle. They demanded a change in the unequal trading rules and the creation of new institutions that were more in line with their objectives. They attempted to change the trade regime in operation, and were controlled by the developed countries. As Stephen Krasner has observed, the DCs then approved rules that subjected them to an authoritarian allocation of resources rather than the rules of the market. They then demanded a limitation of property rights for non-state players (among whom were the multinationals), and total control of their resources spoiled up to then by the major powers. The results depended on the ability of a country to develop an effective ideological position and a persuasive diplomatic policy.

The change became apparent in the 1980s. A growing number of DCs then turned towards extensive liberalization programmes – the result of several converging elements. Previous models and structural adjustment programmes of the World Bank and the IMF, which had required governments to launch such programmes, had all failed. Integration in the global economy through a rapid liberalization of trade, finance and investments would be a guarantee of economic success.

Thus, as noted by UNCTAD: 'It is expected that a freeing of trade will lead to greater efficiency and competitiveness, and to the necessary export receipts for financing imports and the acquisition of intermediate goods'

(UNCTAD 1994). DCs also thought that opening up to private investment would accelerate economic growth by swelling domestic resources and productivity through the transfer of technology. Such policies were to overcome debt payment difficulties, but also put these countries on the path to sustainable and rapid growth, with the ability to face up to external shocks (UNCTAD 1999).

In 1996, sixty-five DCs adopted ninety-eight liberalization investment measures, whereas in 1991 only thirty-five of them had undertaken such changes. The changes included the opening up of industries to investment that was previously closed to foreigners, abolition of acceptance procedures, and the appearance of stimulants to investment. Measures were also adopted that aimed at encouraging profits, together with taxation instruments that complemented them. Import and export licences were removed. Guinea Conakry adopted price liberalization, international bidding for public purchases, suppression of all public enterprises, closure of state banks, and lifting of import and export restrictions (including the suppression of export taxes, and the pursuit of tariff concessions among external partners in order to diversify the export of Guinean products). The country also introduced a share market auction.

In 1989, Mexico reduced its restrictions on foreign ownership by 100 per cent in three-quarters of the 654 economic sectors. Capital can now be repatriated freely, and no regulation has been imposed on the exchange controls that had been set up to regulate capital transactions.

The changed strategy of developing countries was one of the main reasons for a shift in their attitude *vis-à-vis* the GATT. From being merely passive observers during the negotiations up to the Uruguay Round, DCs became full participants. DCs engaged in trade liberalization strategy and abandoned their reservations towards the GATT, where barriers to international trade were being addressed (Finger and Messerlin 1989: 21). This is not to say that all DCs have the same interests to defend. Certain of them, such as Singapore, Korea, Mexico and Brazil, export diversified products.

The hard core of Brazilian exports to the American and European markets is agricultural and food products (soya, chickens, pigs, rice and coffee), electrical machines and equipment, wood, paper and cellulose, textiles (clothing and household linen) and footwear. Santa Catarina is the fifth export state in Brazil after Sao Paulo, Minas Gerais, Rio Grande do Sul and Paraná, but is in first position for per capita exports. It possesses a territory equivalent in area to that of Belgium (561.4 km^2, corresponding to 7 per cent of the Brazilian coastline) and a rapidly increasing population (4,875,000 inhabitants with an increase of 34.3 per cent between 1986 and 1990). It is the leading producer of household linen in Brazil and accounts for 70 per cent of the Brazilian exports. Its production of ceramics rivals that of Italy, and it is the second producer of coal in Brazil after Rio Grande do Sul.

Other countries, such as China, are at an earlier stage of development and export labour-intensive industrial products. Others again, such as Panama and the Bahamas, export services. Finally, with regard to agricultural products, certain countries are exporters of tropical and others of temperate products. But the DCs also have interests in common. They are weak compared with the major powers, and therefore need a system with strict rules as protection against them. Whenever Japan, the USA or the European Union have trade differences, they have the unilateral power to impose their point of view. But when the USA has a disagreement with Nicaragua or Zimbabwe, the situation is unbalanced and the small country lacks the means to resist (Krueger 1999: 911).

DCs have submitted to WTO rules, and increased the percentage of their consolidated tariffs from 21 to 73 per cent (Srinavasan 1999: 1053). The Multifibre Agreement was dismantled and agriculture was submitted to WTO discipline. Concerning market access, however, the balance is unfavourable to them (UNCTAD 1994: 4). Most of the tariff reductions have taken place on industrial products, and these do not figure among their principal exports. In developed countries, tariff reductions on industrial products approach 38 per cent, but only 34 per cent for DCs (ibid.). Tariff reductions are not directed towards products exported from DCs, but especially towards those from developed countries (from 43 to 62 per cent).

Despite eight rounds of negotiations, many tariff peaks remain in certain sectors, such as textiles, agricultural and manufactured products. In Canada, customs duties on milk products are 600 per cent, and the USA levies 132 per cent on peanut butter, from 14 to 32 per cent on wool, cotton and synthetic fibres, as well as 179 per cent on powdered milk. Japan levies 550 per cent customs duties on rice, and the EU, 215 per cent on frozen beef, as well as between 46 to 215 per cent on fruit juices. Developing countries are not exempt from high customs duties.

The Uruguay Round and developing countries – substantial results

The impact of the Uruguay Round on DCs has been particularly prominent on the new issues under negotiation. Intellectual property is a striking example, since the protection granted has consequences for transnational investment decisions. This area is even more important in that the DCs are users rather than initiators of technological innovations. One consequence of these agreements has been to increase the price of certain pharmaceutical products and the licences awarded to DCs. On the other hand, protection of intellectual property rights can also offer certain benefits to them; they have an advantage in the area of geographical indication. In the debates over whether basmati rice originates from India or Pakistan or tequila from Mexico, these countries have derived substantial advantages from protecting their resources, just as France and Switzerland have gained from protecting champagne and Gruyère cheese. Textiles are also an interesting example. Many of the 'African' fabrics that are found on the European and American markets are imitations of those from Mauritania and Senegal, without the latter having been able to profit from their inventions. A protection system must also be envisaged for bio-technology, for a large number of developing countries could improve their status by promoting their genetic resources.

One of the great achievements of the Uruguay Round was to enable agriculture to be subjected to WTO discipline. Agriculture forms a particularly important sector for DCs, which can be classified into three groups. The first are exporters of tropical products, the second are exporters of temperate products (Argentina, Thailand), and the third are importers of agricultural products. These groups overlap. Certain Sub-Saharan countries export tropical products but import foodstuffs, but the main division remains between the importers and exporters. DCs have concentrated on suppressing the export subsidies that they also, moreover, have to respect.

But, as Anne Krueger affirms, these subsidies would be more useful in other economic sectors (1999: 920). This suppression could introduce a rise in the prices of agricultural products, which has not been noted, moreover. DCs are subject to lower reductions than developed countries: 24 per cent over a period of ten years, and exemption for the least developed. They are also authorized to employ internal support measures, which are not permitted for developed countries. Direct and indirect investments and subsidies for the poorest farmers are excluded from the total sum of support measures (Michalopoulos 1999: 6), which are in any case subject to the 'peace' clause and the 'Green Boxes'.

DCs would benefit from a greater liberalization of agriculture, and should therefore ally themselves to the Cairns Group, as some in fact did under the Uruguay Round. They should follow the aim of a more substantial reduction in export subsidies and an improvement in market access, while defending the subsidies that have been granted to various agricultural groups. Export subsidies are sufficiently important for DCs for them to be included in the Millennium Action Plan that the African leaders discussed in 2001. This plan should be endorsed by the Organization of African Unity (OAU), as it was at the July 2001 G8 Summit in Genoa 2001 (*The Economist*, 7 July 2001). The special provisions for developing countries are discussed in Table 12.1.

Table 12.1 Special provisions for developing countries

Subject	Provisions
Institutional	Additional time Technical assistance
Tariffs	Consolidation of ceilings platforms at the highest level (25–30 per cent) Fewer concessions offered by the DCs
Agriculture	Lower reductions on the non-tariff barriers and internal support measures – about two-thirds of those of developed countries Longer transition periods – ten years instead of six and a much greater numbers of subsidies permitted DCs are exempt from the annual notification of their support measures and from the reduction of export subsidies and internal support measures
Textiles	Special treatment of the LDCs, small suppliers and fibre-producing countries
Safeguards	No safeguarding measures for low volume imports – representing not more than 3 per cent of total imports and more than 9 per cent of all imported goods from the DCs Maintaining the measures for a maximum of ten years instead of eight Possibility of reapplying measures more frequently
Subsidies	Elimination of the export subsidies in eight years Exemptions for countries whose GNP is less than US$1,000 Elimination period of seven years for transition countries, but with flexibility for measures necessary for transforming planned economies into those in the free market category Provisions *de minimis* for export markets
Anti-dumping	Special provisions for DCs Provisions *de minimis*
TRIMs	Longer elimination periods (five years for DCs, seven years for countries in transition and LDCs) Possibility of extension, case by case
TRIPs	Longer transitions for adjustment – five years for DCs and economies in transition, eleven years for the LDCs
Balance of payments	Technical assistance Simplified consultations for the LDCs
Services	Principle of progressive participation for the DCs; less opening for desired sectors Fewer provisions for financial services

Table 12.1 continued

Subject	Provisions
Technical barriers to trade	Technical assistance for adjusting to international standards and technical standards in the export markets
Sanitary and phytosanitary measures	Technical assistance by international institutions (Codex, WHO, CIPV)
	Developed countries should take account of the specific needs of the DCs when applying sanitary and phytosanitary measures

Source: UNCTAD (1995: 27).

Developed countries undertook to submit 16 per cent of their textile imports to WTO discipline, but the Textile Agreement did not specify the distribution of the articles that had to be integrated. The developed countries, taking advantage of this loophole, were able to choose the products to be integrated and did this in accordance with the restrictions they had imposed before the agreement. Clothing that formed the main exports of DCs only constituted a small part of the products subjected to liberalization. As Table 12.2 indicates, the integration process still only achieved very modest results.

The Agreement on Services was of great interest to DCs, since they realized that services were important for the growth of their economies, and financial services served as a stimulant for their exports. DCs enjoyed a comparative advantage in the service sectors that were either markedly labour-intensive, or required highly qualified technical personnel. Having regard to these two factors, the DCs were able to increase their services in enterprises relative to construction and engineering, distribution, education, and health services, as well as those employed in tourism, travel, recreation, cultural and sporting activities, and transport. The situation for these

Table 12.2 Percentage of clothing in relation to the volume of products integrated in Stages 1 and 2

Member state	Percentage
USA	12.4
European Union	7.2
Canada	7.9
Norway	10.6

Source: WTO Doc. G/L/179: 29.

countries was varied. Certain countries only provided a few services, whereas others (among those with a moderate income) had modern and competitive financial services, and consequently had comparative advantages in this sector.

Tourism, for example, is a flourishing industry in many DCs, and also offers a great potential for maritime transport, transport of persons and health. As recalled by Mattoo (1999 :18), the health sector remains an area in which DCs could become one of the principal exporters, either in attracting patients to their hospitals or in sending their doctors abroad. A small number of developing countries, such as Cuba, India and Jordan, are serious competitors. India has very highly qualified doctors, and patients from both developing and developed countries go there for treatment. The costs of coronary by-passes in India are less than in the USA, and certain companies organize packages that include hospital treatment (Gupta and Nunnenkamp 1998: 228–229). SERVIMED, a commercial company, created in Cuba, offers health and tourist packages. In 1995 and 1996, 25,000 patients and 1,500 students went to Cuba for treatment or training, thus contributing US$25 million.

But the DCs are not really on an equal footing in the service sector. A certain number of problems arise concerning market access. Taxes are levied on people through visas and airport taxes, and by customs duties on the goods necessary for the production of films, television programmes, computers and telecommunication equipment. Subsidies are granted by developed countries (construction or communication), and whereas DCs suffer from financial limitations, service enterprises in developed countries are given financial support by their governments. Regulations concerning security and the environment, standardization and recording procedures also tend to limit the participation of developing countries. It is important for DCs to participate in the sectors that have been identified – health, transport and construction – for otherwise it will lead to their exclusion in these sectors.

Access to information channels or distribution networks discriminates against the DCs. Governmental measures (migration measures and procedures, limitations on obtaining travel permits and visas, and recognition of qualifications) lack transparency. Public procurements still remain inaccessible. Services are dominated by a small number of very powerful companies. In tourism, for example, 80 per cent of the market belongs to Thomson, Airtours, First Choice and Thomas Cook. The DC service providers, for the most part, small and medium-sized enterprises, have to compete with multinationals that have great financial strength and access to the latest technologies. The latest mergers and takeovers, and the strategic alliances have an impact on competition; integration between tour operators and travel agencies, for example, put DCs in a bad position, in that it is difficult for them to gain access to such alliances. Article IX clauses must be reinforced in respect of the misuse of a dominant position, notification and restrictive practices of the private sector, and insistence on the principles favourable to competition.

The DC commitments have been fewer in number than those of developed countries, and have not been consolidated (see Table 12.3). The Agreement on Services enables DCs to choose the sectors that they wish to open.

Table 12.3 Structure of the commitments by the WTO members

Sectors	Number of members	Member states
Below 20	44	Angola, Bahrein, Barbados, Benin, Botswana, Burkina Faso, Cameroon, Central African Republic, Chad, Congo, Republic of Congo, Costa Rica, Cyprus, Fiji, Gabon, Guinea, Guinea-Bissau, Guyana, Haiti, Honduras, Madagascar, Malawi, Maldives, Mali, Malta, Mauritania, Mauritius, Mozambique, Myanmar, Namibia, Niger, Paraguay, Rwanda, St Kitts and Nevis, St Lucia, St Vincent and Grenadines, Solomon Islands, Sri Lanka, Surinam, Swaziland, Tanzania, Togo, Uganda, Zambia
21–40	23	Bangladesh, Bolivia, Brunei Dar-es-Salaam, Burundi, Côte d'Ivoire, Djibouti, San Domingo, El Salvador, Ghana, Grenada, Guatemala, Kenya, Macao, Mongolia, Nigeria, Papua New Guinea, Peru, Qatar, Senegal, Sierra Leone, Tunisia, Uruguay, Zimbabwe
41–60	10	Antigua and Barbuda, Belize, Cuba, India, Morocco, Netherlands Antilles, Nicaragua, Pakistan, Trinidad and Tobago, Arab Emirates
81–100	24	Argentina, Brazil, Chile, Czech Republic, Dominican Republic, Ecuador, Egypt, Hong Kong, Indonesia, Israel, Jamaica, Kuwait, Lesotho, Liechtenstein, New Zealand, Panama, Poland, Romania, Singapore, Slovakia, Slovenia, South Africa, Turkey, Venezuela
101–120	8	Australia, Bulgaria, Canada, Gambia, Estonia, Philippines, Switzerland, Thailand
More than 120	11	Colombia, EU (15), Hungary, Iceland, Japan, Korea, Kyrgyz Republic, Malaysia, Mexico, Norway, USA

Source: WTO document S/C/W/95, 9 February 1999, p. 11.

The greatest conflict between the developed countries and DCs concerned the movement of persons. Substantial progress was made in the movement of qualified persons, especially intra-company staff, business visitors and, to a lesser extent, independent professions. The agreement did not apply to the temporary movements of service providers. Commitments by many countries ensured a greater freedom of movement for temporary workers travelling abroad without requiring a commercial presence (Mukherjee 1999: 91). Developing countries were not very active in this field. The agreement does not define temporary residences, but the commitment lists indicate visiting periods from 30 days to five years. Countries grant these periods according to the categories of those concerned. Most frequently, the business visitor on a mission is granted from 30 to 90 days. The agreement is not to the advantage of the DCs, because it applies mainly to qualified workers rather than those with average or few qualifications. Of the thirteen indus-trialized countries that made commitments in this area, twelve approved the entry of qualified personnel, whereas out of seventy-two DCs, only forty-three opened their frontiers to qualified staff. Commitments in this field concerned the transfer of company staff, business visitors and independent professionals.

The DCs tried to obtain concessions for a greater number of professional categories, and it is therefore in this domain that new negotiations must be arranged in order to restore the balance in favour of the DCs.

The shortfall for the DCs is particularly evident in the mechanism for the dispute settlements. The legal subtleties and technical nature of the issues make the defence of a complaint a complex task. Developed countries have a multitude of lawyers at their disposal to act in their defence, but – except for some cases – DCs do not have the same means. Brazil mobilized its political and financial resources when the government lodged a complaint against the treatment of their chicken imports by the EU, but the government had the banks behind it and could send its best experts. When the DCs engage the services of lawyers, they can easily find themselves in the same situation as the banana producers in the Caribbean, whose lawyers were prevented from attending the meetings, because they were not high-ranking civil servants (Croome 1998: 18). As Burtless *et al.* affirm, the WTO defends the interests of the USA, for the dispute settlement body acts, either in support of the USA or in arranging that the accused offer favourable concessions (1998: 101). Working parties and the regulatory organ often pronounce interpretations that restrain the rights of the DCs. Examples abound: the case of oil from Venezuela; woolen shirts from India; or the case of the tortoise and shrimps between the USA, India, Malaysia, Pakistan and Thailand.

Imbalance of power acts to the disadvantage of the weakest. Countries must apply the recommendations and conclusions of the Dispute Settlement

Body (DSB), but a country may in sensitive cases hesitate to do this. Its only recourse then is to adopt retaliatory measures, but they may find this difficult when up against powerful countries (Lal das 1999: 157). The USA or EU can permit themselves to disregard the DSB conclusions, since the costs incurred are minimal – except for those that prejudice the credibility of the organization, as in the case of the EU banana imports or the meat with hormones (Rodrik 1995: 51).

Nevertheless, since 1995 – with the exception of the Sub-Saharan countries – the DCs have increasingly resorted to the dispute settlement mechanism. Of 219 complaints addressed to this body, more than 26 per cent of the cases were introduced by the DCs (some examples are shown in Table 12.4). About two-thirds of the disputes involved a developing country (Footer 2001: 56).

DCs participated as plaintiff, defendant or third party. The number of complaints from the DCs was thus increased (see Table 12.5).

DCs have longer transition periods available to them, more flexibility in the application of the agreements, and a special status within the dispute settlement mechanism (see Table 12.6). The Director General may offer his good services in a complaint laid by a DC against a developed country, and member countries must pay special attention to the problems and interests of DCs. Chile used this clause during a complaint against the EU denouncing its discriminatory attitude in the import of 'coquilles saint Jacques'.

DCs are allowed more time for consultations and in the application of the DSB conclusions, and may require that one of the working party members has to be from a developing country (Article 8.10). Indonesia demanded nine extra months in order to apply the measures, arguing that its automobile industry needed a period of structural adjustment. The WTO Secretariat is under obligation to give all necessary assistance to the DCs, but according to the latter this has been of little help. In certain cases, DCs have been successful in disputes with the major powers. The first case raised by Costa Rica against safeguard measures adopted by the USA against cotton and fibre textile was successful, but, during a similar case, the USA decided

Table 12.4 Summary of appearance of DCs in disputes

Groups of countries	Plaintiff (%)	Defendant (%)
All DCs	70.9	56.2
DCs	26.3	40.6
LDCs	0	0

Source: Park and Umbricht (2001: 16).

Table 12.5 Complaints laid with the WTO

Groups of countries	Participants	Non-participants
DCs	South Africa, Barbados, Belize, Bolivia, Cameroon, Chile, Colombia, Costa Rica, Côte d'Ivoire, Cuba, Dominican Republic, Ecuador, Egypt, El Salvador, Ghana, Grenada, Guatemala, Honduras, India, Indonesia, Israel, Jamaica, Nicaragua, Nigeria, Pakistan, Panama, Paraguay, Peru, Philippines, San Domingo, St Lucia, St Vincent and Grenadian, Senegal, Sri Lanka, Surinam, Swaziland, Trinidad and Tobago, Uruguay, Venezuela, Zimbabwe	Antigua et Barbados, Bahrain, Botswana, Brunei, Congo, Cyprus, Dar-es-Salaam, Arab Emirates, Fiji, Gabon, Guyana, Mauritius, Jordan, Kenya, Kuwait, Macao, Malta, Mongolia, Morocco, Namibia, Papua, New Guinea, Oman, Qatar, St Kitts, St Christopher and Nevis, Tunisia,
LDCs		Angola, Bangladesh, Benin, Burkina Faso, Burundi, Djibouti, Gambia, Guinea, Guinea Bissau, Haiti, Solomon Islands, Lesotho, Madagascar, Malawi, Maldives, Mali, Mauritania, Mozambique, Myanmar, Niger, Uganda, Central African Republic, Republic of the Congo, Rwanda, Sierra Leone, Tanzania, Chad, Togo, Zambia

Source: Park and Umbricht (2001: 15).

Table 12.6 WTO disputes as of 1 February 2000

Plaintiff	Defendant	Complaint
Venezuela/Brazil	USA	Standard for refined oil
Costa Rica	USA	Restrictions on the import of cotton and fibre underwear
India	USA	Measures affecting the import of woven shirts and blouses
Brazil	EU	Measures affecting the import of poultry
Malaysia/Pakistan/ Thailand	USA	Banning the import of shrimps and products based on shrimps

Table 12.6 continued

Plaintiff	Defendant	Complaint
Brazil	Canada	Banning the import of shrimps and products based on shrimps
Korea	USA	Anti-dumping duty rights on Megabyte DRAMS
Brazil	Canada	Measures affecting the export of civil aircraft
India	EU	Anti-dumping rights against the import of cotton bed-linen
Korea	USA	Anti-dumping measures against steel
Brazil	EU	Measures affecting differentiated and favourable treatment of coffee
India	EU	Anti-dumping investigations concerning bleached cotton
India	EU	Measures affecting the import of rice
Argentina	EU	Quota against the import of nuts
Panama/Ecuador/ Guatemala/ Honduras/Mexico	EU	Import regime for the sale and distribution of bananas
Chile	USA	Compensatory measures against the import of salmon
Colombia	USA	Safeguarding measures against the import of brooms
India/Malaysia/ Pakistan/Thailand	USA	Banning the import of shrimps and shrimp-based products
Korea	USA	Anti-dumping rights against the import of televisions
Philippines	USA	Banning the import of shrimps and shrimp-based products
DC against DC		
Philippines	Brazil	Measures affecting dehydrated coconuts
Brazil	Peru	Investigation of compensatory measures against bus import
Hungary	Slovakia	Measures affecting customs duties on wheat
India	South Africa	Anti-dumping rights against the import of pharmaceutical products
Indonesia	Argentina	Safeguarding measures against the import of footwear

Source: http://www.wto.org

to withdraw the safeguard measures by alleging that the imports of shirts and blouses had decreased. The most notorious case was that of bananas against the EU. Ecuador requested WTO membership in order to enjoy the advantage of the dispute settlement mechanism.

The WTO agreements allow for technical assistance to be given to DCs and LDCs, notably in the area of technical barriers to trade, sanitary and phytosanitary measures, evaluation of customs duties, inspection prior to despatch, dispute settlements, review of trade policies and of intellectual property rights. Developing countries are not subject to the same notification requirements, and have greater flexibility in protecting their domestic industries. All the WTO agreements extend the transition periods for the DCs, except for the anti-dumping measures.

The Agreement on Subsidies and Compensatory Measures enables DCs, unlike the other members, to continue subsidising their exports for a certain period of time. They may postpone the implementation of the agreements, especially in the area of intellectual property rights, subsidies and compensatory measures. Developed countries must accelerate the elimination of quotas on textile products from DCs. The agreements arrange special conditions for LDCs, but numerous loopholes exist in certain agreements and act to the disadvantage of the DCs. These arise from the lack of clarity concerning market access, and special and differentiated treatment in favour of DCs. Developed countries admitted that the interests of DCs must be taken into consideration when the agreements were applied, but with the exception of the transition periods, there has been no difference in their application between the developed and developing countries.

13 The emergence of new issues

Following the Marrakech Agreements, developed countries exerted pressure for the inclusion of new subjects on the international agenda, including some that were not exclusively within the commercial domain. The WTO is not the ideal forum for raising these issues, no Article in the GATT mentions social standards, and the social clauses could have been treated by the International Labour Office, for example. The United States (and principally the Democratic Party) were the main precursors in establishing a link between market access and the application of social standards, but similar proposals were also advanced by the political parties in the member states of the EU and by the European Parliament. Kim Elliott observed that the increase in exports to the United States by countries with low wages was at the heart of the debate on social standards (2000: 104), since multinationals would move their activities into countries that applied lower social standards. (DCs, however, considered that protectionism was the principal motive and was opposed to the inclusion of these standards in trade negotiations. The inclusion of social standards is based on five principles and fundamental rights of labour: (1) freedom of association; (2) collective bargaining; (3) limitations on child labour; (4) prohibition of forced labour; and (5) non-discrimination in employment (Wilkinson and Hughes 2000: 261; *Dow Jones Newswires*, 24 July 2001).

Trade and the environment: GMO hormones

For five years, the links between trade and the environment have been the subject of numerous debates in the WTO, and form part of the issues that the developed countries wanted to address in the trade agenda. They have been nourished by numerous disputes that have arisen in international trade. The best known of these are doubtlessly those between the USA and Mexico on the import of tuna fish caught by methods that are harmful to the dolphins, and the issue of shrimps and tortoises between the USA and certain countries

in South-east Asia.[1] The WTO decision in favour of Mexico enraged environmentalists and turned them away from the WTO.

The developed countries reacted to the pressing demands that were made
on them by the environmentalist groups. Developing countries, mainly India
and the South-east Asian countries, were also opposed to the negotiation
of environmental clauses and those concerning social standards. These two
issues were in accordance with the North–South cleavage. The argument
of the DCs was simple – the motives of the developed countries were protectionist. They decided, therefore, to react against the extension of the
discussion on environment to the processes and methods of production
(PMP) (Michalopoulos 1999: 18).

The debate on the links between the environment and trade is complex,
and the liberalization of trade is frequently depicted as being prejudicial
to the environment. But the situation is complicated. It is therefore necessary to examine the relations between the liberalization of trade and the
environment, case by case. There exist areas in which it is to the mutual and
positive advantage of both parties, and others in which there is a conflict.
There are many examples of favourable combinations. Discipline in the area
of subsidies, for example, can lead to a reduction in the use of polluting
products. Increased competition can promote the structural adjustment of
obsolete and protected production methods. Discipline in the area of technical barriers to trade can stimulate trade in ecological products, and subsidies
to services can contribute to a rational allocation of resources (Cotter 2001;
http:/www.itd.org/issues/essays).

In 1971, the GATT set up a working party on environmental measures and
international trade that did not became effective until 1991. The Uruguay
Round negotiation ended with the creation of a Committee on Trade and the
Environment, which identified several issues. Two of these were particularly
important. The first concerned the relations between the WTO and the
environmental agreements put forward in several international precincts.
When environmental agreements are universally applied, no trade problems
arise. But when this is not the case, they can do so.

The effective aim of the GATT/WTO is the liberalization of trade based
on principles such as non-discrimination and national treatment, but the
environmental agreements envisage environmental protection by means
of trade restrictions, and these restrictions are stricter for those who are
non-members of the agreements. These provisions clearly conflict with the
principle of non-discrimination, as is illustrated by the Montreal Protocol.
This recommends an embargo on the import and export of products containing or produced by controlled substances, and forbids the import of
methyl bromide by non-member countries of the protocol (Rutgers 1999:
66).[2] The second problem concerns technical standards, packaging and

labelling adopted by developed countries in order to maintain their environmental status. The DCs claim that the standards adopted by the North frequently result in a decline in their exports, since labelling reduces the competitiveness of non-labelled products. Imports of paper from Brazil, for example, have declined since the introduction of a label by the EU (De Motta *et al*. 1997: 66–79).

Labelling programmes are allied to the lifecycle of products and their production processes (use of energy, air, soil and water), and are therefore susceptible to disadvantaging imported products in relation to those produced locally. Many disputes arising within the WTO concern production methods and processes. The USA maintains that these PMP are subject to WTO disciplines, but this is denied by DCs (Raghavan 1996: 11).

WTO rules concerning technical barriers to trade can give rise to numerous disputes (Markandya 1997: 29). Although the GATT rules do not allow a country to impose its domestic laws on another country – if only to protect the health or natural resources there (principle of extra-nationality) – the WTO has never adopted the results of the working party on the case of tuna and dolphins between the USA (supported by the EU) and Mexico. The results enraged the environmentalists, who concluded that the WTO was favouring trade rules at the expense of those for the environment, and this would work against the protection of the planet. From the ecological point of view, the prejudice resulting from a product or its production process is part of the same problem. The WTO should have given a ruling against the massacre of the dolphins and not about the tuna, but the ruling was according to the legal and commercial criteria that pay little attention to environmental issues.

The Agreement on Sanitary and Phytosanitary Measures could give rise to numerous disputes in the future. Some have already arisen, as was the case between the USA and the EU on the use of growth hormones for raising cattle, or between Canada and Australia on the import of salmon.[3] At the heart of the problem is the requirement for scientific evidence, which could give rise to numerous controversies. But the type of evidence and how far it can be employed are points that are far from being decided. When the evidence is insufficient, the agreement authorizes member states to adopt provisional measures based on the precautionary principle. The application of these measures by the EU is quite strict, and the considerable use it has made of them has produced disputes between the USA and the EU.

These disputes could also arise in the future over the sensitive subject of genetically modified products. Genetic modification of crops and plants makes them resistant to pesticides and diseases, and in this sense may be favourable to the environment. But it is not yet certain whether these manipulations are injurious or not to human health. According to Perdikis *et al*., the Agreements on the WTO and on the Sanitary and Phytosanitary

Measures are equipped to deal with the GMO (2001: 385). The agreements seek to limit the protection enjoyed by local producers, but other groups have emerged from among the environmentalists and consumers to which the governments cannot reply. The governments thus are unable to claim that they are unaware of their commitment towards the WTO when confronted by pressure groups. According to the authors, the case of hormone beef illustrates the difficulty of using rules directed towards the producer in order to respond to the pressures of consumers and environmentalists. Those against the use of GMOs opposed the liberal approach of the WTO and found an issue capable of mobilizing a whole myriad of groups, consumers and environmentalists in their wake (Runge and Jackson 2000: 113). The WTO has done nothing to counter these attacks.

The EU possesses two texts on GMOs. The 90/220 Directive obliges importers to notify EU member states whenever they put GMO products on the market. The 95/95 Directive imposes labelling of products containing GMOs, implemented in 2004. These directives filter new products and the EU decides case by case. The EU has now suspended any new demand for GMO authorization on the Community market. Among eleven products from the USA submitted for authorization, only five have been approved. The United States and Canada have a more liberal approach, and the consumers are less cautious than their European counterparts where the purchase of GMO products is concerned. In 1998, more than 500 varieties of GMO plants were available in the USA, and GMO soya and cotton occupied more than 28 per cent of the cultivated land. In Canada, GMO crops covered an area of more than 100,000 ha. In 1997, Switzerland launched an initiative on GMOs, seeking to restrict their sale, but this was refused because it was associated with genetic modifications in the medical domain. Consumers allowed the use of genetic technology in medicine, whereas they rejected it in foodstuffs. The majority of European consumers have refused the use of GMOs.

Certain companies have changed their policy because of pressure from consumers. Unilever and Cadbury have suspended the use of GMOs in their products. Nestlé has resorted to labelling, in order to give consumers freedom of choice (Runge and Jackson 2000: 391). Producers who put products containing no GMOs on the market, such as Ben and Jerry (ibid.: 116), have seen their sales triple in the space of a few years. But labelling does not constitute a panacea for the GMOs, because it identifies neither the quantity of the GMO in the product, nor which GMO is concerned. Nevertheless, the USA hesitated to drag the EU before the WTO Dispute Settlement Body, because they feared losing the case under European consumer pressure, and finding themselves faced by the same legal disputes as the tobacco companies (Interview Commission of the EU, DG Trade, Brussels, July 2000). However, they finally did so in 2004.

Most of the developed countries have demanded that the provision of the environmental agreements should not be challenged by the WTO (Croome 1998: 37; http://www.wto.org), and the EU has proposed that Article XX (b) of the GATT should serve as a guarantee. This Article, the only one in the Agreement that concerns the environment, authorizes measures directed towards the protection of human beings, plants and health, on condition that they are not applied in a way that discriminates against countries or hinders international trade. DCs demand greater flexibility and the possibility of challenging environmental agreements. They are faced with a choice: either to negotiate an agreement that would limit the abuses by developed countries; or to content themselves with Article XX (b) of the GATT and have recourse to the dispute regulation mechanism in order to counter the violations of the developed countries.

Competition: a North–South cleavage

Competition is also an issue that certain countries would like included on the agenda. In 1996, following the ministerial meeting in Singapore, the WTO set up a working party on trade and competition. Several aspects of competition already figured in certain WTO agreements, such as trade policy, subsidies, intellectual property rights, and market access for services (Hoekman 2000; http://www.wto.org). As Maskus (2000b: 155) affirms: 'The language of the TRIPS [Trade-Related Intellectual Property Rights] introduces competition policy directly into the WTO, and invites Member States to develop rules that cover the maintenance of competition.' Competition covers many factors, including the control of mergers, dominant market positions, cartels, related sales and other conduct in restraint of trade.

Countries are divided according to a North–South cleavage, but also between the DCs and the USA, which still refuses negotiation on competition. The latter may envisage a limited agreement on competition policies at national level, provided with an authority having the power to apply anti-trust laws, even if this implies extra-territorial application, but they are afraid of seeing their legislation closely examined by an international organization. Japan and the Asian countries are more interested in knowing whether the WTO rules are relative to the promotion of competition and to addressing market distortions. They recognize that protecting the market by frontier regulation is no longer possible in a globalized world.

Influenced by the merger between McDonnell Douglas and Boeing, the EU has urged the WTO to look into the competition and mergers that affect the world markets. According to Carolyn Rhodes (independent of the WTO), the European Commissioners have increased their visibility and entrepreneurial intentions on the international economic stage (Rhodes 1999: 170).

The WTO is well placed to treat the international aspects of competition, including the relevant laws and their application. According to the EU, all countries are interested in receiving the benefits of liberalization and in the elimination of barriers erected by companies to protect their dominant position.

DCs accept these views and consider that competition should primarily be concerned with the behaviour of enterprises, but do not have the power to apply extraterritoriality as the USA would like them to do. DCs have an interest in adopting laws that are directed towards a liberal policy, especially in relation to investments. They already suffer from the effects of mergers that end in the creation of global firms, and are therefore interested in these negotiations.

DCs advocate special and differentiated treatment and protection for their small and medium-sized firms, as well as long transition periods (Shahin 1997: 198–200). An agreement that concentrated purely on anti-trust laws would be of little use to them (Michalopoulos 1999: 18). For small DCs, an open and liberal investment regime would be enough to control problems of restrictive business practices. Few DCs possess these laws, and without them the ability to implement is often limited. Table 13.1 shows the state of play in the adoption of laws on competition.

The priority of DCs is to establish competition policies that are focused on promoting the establishment of companies, elimination of administrative barriers and the reduction in transport costs that are favourable to the creation of dominant positions. The main development problem for DCs lies in the activity of transnationals, which have the potential to dominate the market and can reduce their profits by price fixing and inter-firm transactions. Unless these activities are subject to the proposed rules on competition – which has never been the case up to the present – the DCs have no interest in concentrating on a new competition regime (Michalopoulos 1999: 20). Foreign investment is more crucial for developing countries. The GATT has had this under consideration since the 1980s, and investments were among the new topics for the Uruguay Round.

More recently, the question arose as to whether an agreement was to be negotiated within the WTO or within the Organization for Economic Cooperation and Development (OECD), but an investment regime must take account of the interest of both DCs and transnational firms. The Multilateral Agreement on Investments (MAI) was limited because of opposition from the DCs.

No consensus has been reached as to how competition should be negotiated within the WTO, but several approaches are possible. These range from simple consultations to a harmonization, and the prescription of anti-competitive activities. The first approach would involve the establishment

Table 13.1 The adoption of laws on competition

Country	Date adopted	Country	Date adopted	Country in the course of adopting laws
Africa				
Algeria	1995	Mali	1992	Egypt
Côte d'Ivoire	1991	South Africa	1979	Jordan
Kenya	1988	Tunisia	1991	Gabon
				Ghana
				Morocco
				Senegal
				Zambia
				Zimbabwe
Asia				
China	1993	Sri Lanka	1987	Indonesia
India	1969; 1991	Taiwan	1991	Malaysia
Pakistan	1970	Thailand	1979	Philippines
Latin America				
Argentina	1919; 1946	Jamaica	1993	Ecuador
	1980 in revision	Mexico	1992	El Salvador
Brazil	1962; 1994	Peru	1991; 1994	Paraguay
Chile	1959; 1973	Venezuela	1992	
Colombia	1959; 1992			
Transitional economies				
Belarus	1992	Latvia	1991	Albania
Bulgaria	1991	Moldavia	1982	Armenia
Czech Republic	1991	Poland	1990	Azerbaijan
Estonia	1993	Romania	1991	Croatia
Georgia	1992 in revision	Russia	1991	Macedonia
Hungary	1990	Slovakia	1994	Tajikistan
Kazakhstan	1991; 1994	Ukraine	1992	
Khirgizia	1994	Uzbekistan	1992; 1994	

Source: Hoekman (2000).

of anti-trust standards that would prohibit certain practices while requiring notification of others, and would be administered by the national authorities. The second would link the competition policy to limits in the employment of other WTO practices (anti-dumping). And, finally, to extend the WTO rules, especially Article XXIII of the GATT, in order to enable the Member States to challenge practices that, although not illegal, have resulted in neutralizing the benefits negotiated in the trade agreements. Experts are in agreement that liberalization involves a large number of government policies, including arrangements concerning public procurements, control of improper practices in technical standards and dominant positions, a reduction in subsidies, and a control of restrictive business practices.

The WTO certainly possesses advantages for the setting up of a body of uniform rules, and it also has the Dispute Settlement Body to impose discipline for improper behaviour – the OECD is less well equipped to confront competition. Some people, however, are of the opinion that in order to treat competition it would be enough to reinforce the dispute settlement mechanism, and the Kodak and Fuji dispute serves to confirm this.[4]

The Multilateral Agreement on Investments (MAI)

The aim of the OECD in furthering an agreement on investments and in removing all restrictions on them was to ensure that they were treated by the national authorities as though they were local investments. The member states agreed on a broad definition of investments that exceeded the traditional approach, in order to encompass all tangible and intangible assets, and the preparatory operations that even preceded the investment. The definition thus embraced intellectual property and portfolio investment.

The Multilateral Agreement on Investments was to be concluded in 1997, and then in 1998, but it was abandoned shortly afterwards. Some members of the US Congress were unable to support an agreement that did not concern expropriations. In France and Canada, the interest groups mobilized to protect the media and means of communication, the cultural exception having already been negotiated in the NAFTA and WTO (Landau 2001: 122). The DCs, trade unions and environmentalists united against the MAI. The developing countries, under the initiative of India and Malaysia, were opposed to an agreement that they could not have a hand in shaping (Ganesan 1998). They criticized the definition of investments adopted by the OECD and that of national treatment, because the granting of national treatment in the preparatory phase of the investment would remove all flexibility in the conduct of national policy. India considered that the bilateral and regional agreements granted sufficient stability to investments and stimulants.

'Public Citizen', moreover, appropriated a first draft of the treaty in 1997, and published it on the Web, and very soon more than 600 organizations in seventy countries had distributed the report and had denounced it. Their criticisms included the principles of national treatment and non-discrimination applied to investors, the prohibition of performance criteria, the measures that eliminated national laws that conflicted with the MAI standards, the exclusion of non-compensated expropriations, the limitations on the repatriation of profits and other restrictions on the movement of capital, and the dispute settlement mechanisms favourable to investors

(Warkentin and Mingst 2000: 243). But, as Kobrin remarked, the anti-MAI forces alone could not have contributed to the failure of the MAI, for the preamble of the treaty contained no less than seventeen notes expressing reservations by the participants (in Warkentin and Mingst 2000: 243).

The WTO proposals concerning an agreement on investments differ from those of the MAI in respect of the definition of investments, settlement of dispute, problems of social and environmental standards, and the entry and residence of temporary personnel. Table 13.2 recapitulates the main differences between the MAI and the WTO. The WTO work schedule includes linkages between trade and investment, trade measures affecting investments, and comparisons between bilateral, regional and multilateral agreements. Investments had in fact already been included in a certain number of agreements, such as that on services, investments, subsidies and compensatory measures. But the Agreement on Services does not deal with investments as such, although it concerns the resort to investments

Table 13.2 Differences between the MAI and the WTO

Subject	MAI	WTO proposals
Definition of investment	All forms of assets possessed or controlled by an investor, such as company shares (direct or indirect portfolio), bonds and loans, intellectual property rights	Limited to foreign investment, i.e. a certain percentage of participation in the enterprise that enables the entrepreneur to exercise control of his or her enterprise
Performance requirements	Exclusion of requirements (local content, export performance, transfer of technology imposed upon investors)	Requirements must be balanced in such a way as not to create distortions and to be reviewed in the light of developments
Entry and temporary residence of personnel	Right of entry and residence subject to certain exceptions	Covered by the Agreement on Services
Labour and environmental issues	Commitment in the preamble, undertaking not to minimize social standards in order to attract investment	The WTO should take account of the requirements laid down by civil society concerning the responsibilities of the investor *vis-à-vis* the impact on labour and the environment
Scale of development	Not covered	Scale should be included

Source: WTO Secretariat.

as a means of delivering services by means of a trade presence. The USA is reticent about introducing the MAI into the WTO.

For the USA and Canada, the OECD is a small club of developed countries and the forum for privileged negotiation in order to channel national policies, even if it has shown itself to be incapable of transferring the adopted regimes onto the international agenda. The member states of the OECD are the principal sources of investment, but the EU prefers the WTO because the Commission negotiates for its member states, whereas in the OECD all member states negotiate for themselves. The developing countries do not feel ready to negotiate investments within the WTO, but they are henceforth confronted by multilateral rules governing transnationals and access to investments, and have liberalized their trade practices in order to encourage foreign investment. But is the WTO really the suitable forum for treating investment? Would the World Bank not be an acceptable alternative (Shahin 1997: 187)?

The Cancún Summit

Four years after the Seattle Summit failed, the Cancún Summit collapsed in disarray. It should have been the summit of the poor as it aimed to implement the Declaration of Doha, look for new orientations for special and differential treatment, free up farm trade, slash remaining tariffs on industrial goods and give a new impulse to the negotiations. Many issues concerning the developing countries should have been settled in Cancún. According to the World Bank, a successful Doha Round could have raised poor countries' income by US$350 billion a year (*The Economist*, 20 September 2003).

However, agreement has been difficult to find on the different issues of the negotiation. Divisions among members proved too deep. Member states agreed to three areas in agriculture: access to markets, internal support and export subsidies, and to include the special and differential treatment in the agricultural negotiations. Yet, contrary to what had been agreed in August, export subsidies were not to be eliminated.

The result is that almost all developing nations have become more assertive in trade negotiations. The non-governmental organizations (NGOs) played an important role in persuading them to block the progress of talks in order to protect their interests. A group of developing countries, led by Brazil, India and China, the so-called G21, denounced the lack of willingness of the developed countries.

Encouraged by NGO, such as Oxfam, a group of West African countries succeeded in including cotton on the agenda. Their production is hit by rich country subsidies, particularly US subsidies, which depress world prices and the global market. The draft text did not mention eliminating subsidies or obtaining compensation. Some argued that a narrow focus of cotton subsidies alone would not result in the medium- or long-term development of the cotton industry in West Africa. Many African countries refused to negotiate the four new Singapore issues – trade and investment, trade and competition, transparency in government procurement and trade facilitation, while the EU would not budge. The EU retreated but too late. The Cancún Summit failed because of the intransigence of both rich and poor countries. Some countries said that there was no conensus on any of the four issues and they should refer back to working groups in Geneva. Other countries wanted to launch the negotiations in Cancú while other countries were prepared to search for solutions between the two options.

A certain number of issues had to be tackled, such as the phasing out of tariff peaks and escalation had be examined by ministers. Many tariffs continue to impede developing countries' exports, and they have to be phased out. The Agreement on Intellectual Property Rights gives a higher level of protection for the geographical indications, even in the case of disloyal competition.[5] A large number of countries want to negotiate on this.

Also found in the framework of the Agreement on Intellectual Property Rights is the protection of traditional knowledge, important for developing countries and the relations between the agreement and the United Nations Convention on Biodiversity. Other agreements should be examined with respect to anti-dumping rules. These practices are increasing and a large number of developing countries are using them. Sanitary and phytosanitary measures should be revised, notably the principle of precaution which has been used by the EU.

Eastern African countries participated actively in the negotiations, by tabling proposals, notably in the area of special and differential treatment. They were recognized as full participants in the negotiations. They had to table common positions, as they did at the Dakar Summit in July 2003. They should be able to ally themselves with transnational organizations. These movements were beneficial in other negotiations, such as on the environment. Developing countries should obtain advantages due to special and differential treatment. Very few countries are opposed on this issue. Moreover, by conceding on a number of issues, developing countries should be able to gain in other issues. They should make more concessions in services as they have comparative advantages, notably in the area of health and tourism.

It is difficult for the WTO to tackle the problem of development although it is linked to trade. Trade is the engine of growth as are foreign investments. Yet development problems are on the forefront of the international scene. Globalization increased the gap between developed and developing countries, by increasing their marginalization. It is a real challenge for the WTO to become a developmentalist organization.

14 Conclusion

The Uruguay Round negotiations distinguished themselves from earlier ones by their complexity. The negotiations that had been on the scene since the Havana Agreements had been interested solely in the trade in goods, for the main objective of the economic governance in place since the Second World War had been to avoid a recurrence of the 1930s' Depression that had led the world to war (Prakash 2000). The Uruguay Round, on the other hand, enlarged the scope of negotiations to include integration in depth, services, intellectual property, and investment; issues that until then had not previously been negotiated, except for a short interlude connected to an international investment code negotiated (without success) by the United Nations and the OECD.

All these negotiations were the outcome of international economic requirements. The Kennedy Round resulted from the formation of the EEC, and the Tokyo Round from the increased use of subsidies and counterfeits that were flooding the market. The Uruguay Round was also in response to the new international economic requirements, especially the emergence of services in international trade, and the importance of intellectual property rights. These issues were obviously promoted by the USA, which had included them in its commercial policy before proceeding to a multilateral policy.

Public opinion has become aware of the impact of the WTO on economic life, and trade policy can no longer be dealt with in secret and hidden from the public eye. In this way, WTO activities have become more politicized, as can be seen from the wave of protests that have accompanied every ministerial meeting. Reacting to their fear of foreign competition, loss of national sovereignty faced with an international organ, and impoverishment of environmental and social standards, protestors reproach the WTO with favouring transnational companies at the expense of other social bodies, and accuse it of a thousand wrongs, from the death of the environment to the exploitation of children.

Voices are raised announcing the demise of the WTO if the organization does not succeed in launching new negotiations. They stress that, if the WTO does not undertake these new negotiations, regionalization will prevail and regional groups will confront each other in a merciless struggle. Other voices are raised because of the division between the WTO and the ecological imperatives. Although it is undeniable that some of the measures adopted by governments under the pretext of ecology are scarcely disguised protectionism and evoke the spectre of eco-protectionism or eco-dumping, these debates cannot be resolved by joining the choir of voices preaching excessive liberalization (Jander and Inotai 1996: 4). The Marrakesh Agreements are not going to inaugurate a new era, and the solution does not lie in using trade sanctions to enforce environmental or social standards, or in a total lack of authority on the part of the WTO.

Other protectionist instruments will be created, for national administrations have always shown considerable creativity in devising new instruments to limit imports. Following each negotiation, they have decreed new laws governing their import regimes and protecting their national industries. The Marrakesh Agreements are also going to be accompanied by a reinforcement of regionalization as a result of the growing globalization of the economy. The GATT had never examined the degree of compatibility between the regional agreements and the trade regime, since the Cold War was at its height, and there was no question then of criticizing the European Community during the Cold War. The WTO is better equipped to face up to regionalism, but it has so far adopted a low profile in this area.

The WTO suffers from a lack of democracy. Caught between the claims of anti-globalists, developing countries and NGOs, it has to escape from the impasse into which Seattle has thrown it. The awakening of DCs has sorely shaken the organization. Critics exploded during the Seattle meeting; DCs accused the WTO of producing one-sided agreements and denounced improper resort to the 'green rooms'. They rejected any inclusion of social rights in the trade agenda, whereas, as Clare Short has underlined, social rights are really more the concern of development than trade (http://www.columbia.edu). The WTO must reserve a place for DCs and NGOs that goes beyond the mere distribution of official documents. It must also accept that NGOs should use their expertise in the dispute settlements, by hearing the *amicus curiae*.

The links between the WTO and globalization are very complex. Globalization reduces the autonomy of governments and limits the changes of them following independent macro-economic policies. The creation of the WTO came about due to globalization, and was an attempt to introduce coordination in trade policies. In a certain way, it forms the counterpart to the Maastricht Agreements for the EU, in the latter's intention to regain control of the instruments of economic policy. Trade is at present between firms and results more from the strategic considerations of transnational enterprises than from national requirements. The transnationals were active in the corridors of the Uruguay Round negotiations. Governments are negotiating directly with the transnationals on the localization of the latter's activities in order to retain high-value industries within their national areas. And when they are not developing infrastructures necessary for their activities, they are granting them subsidies and tax cuts. The links to the WTO therefore go beyond the liberalization resulting from negotiations and enable transnationals to act freely (Ricupero 1998: 24).

The Doha Summit responded to these questions, but this will not be the end of the story – a story that has continued for more than fifty years. The WTO, through its agreements, will continue to play an important role in the future of world trade.

Notes

Introduction

1 In particular, the Gephardt Law contained some embargoes against exports of Toshiba from Japan and some defence equipment from Norway, after it had been disclosed that the two companies were connected with the Soviet Union (Destler 1995: 93).

1 The WTO: from disappointment to hope

1 Originally there were four: the Agreement on Beef and Dairy Products, which only applied to signatories to the agreement. These two agreements were integrated into the Agricultural Agreement and no longer had an independent status.

2 The Agreement on Sanitary and Phytosanitary Measures

1 Many trade problems concerning fish imports caused dissent among members, including a dispute between Canada and Australia involving the import of Canadian salmon.

2 The United States authorizes the use of hormones for raising farm animals. In 1981, the EC banned the use of DES (diethylstilbestrol), a synthetic growth hormone used in cattle foodstuffs. Its reasons were based on maintaining the tradition of natural feeding of cattle and the prevention of any effect of this hormone on human beings. Certain reports indicated a correlation between the use of hormones and growth in humans. While remaining scientifically unproven, these reports supported a feeling of risk. In 1989, the EC banned the import of cattle fed with this hormone. The EC maintained that the embargo was founded on considerations of health and not of trade. In June 1995, the United States and Canada appealed to the WTO, alleging that the embargo constituted a disguised restriction on international trade, that it was based neither on existing international standards nor upon an evaluation of the risks, and that the decision lacked scientific basis. In August 1996, the special group set up by the Appeal Organ for settling WTO disputes published its report, according to which the ban imposed by the EC on meat and meat products originating from animals treated with certain hormones for anabolic purposes contravened the Agreement on Sanitary and Phytosanitary Measures (Articles 3.1, 5.1 and 5.5). In September

1997, the EC appealed. The result, made public in January 1998, reverted to the previous conclusions concerning certain sections of the agreement.

The Appeal Organ did not share the opinion of the special group concerning the violation of Article 3.1 in maintaining, without justification in respect of Article 3.3, SPS (Sanitary and Phytosanitary Standards) measures that are not laid down on the basis of international standards. The Appeal Organ insisted on the fact that, by virtue of Article 3.3, WTO members have the autonomous right to set up a level of protection higher than that defined by existing international standards relative to the health of persons when there is a scientific justification permitting such action. The Appeal Organ confirmed the violation of Article 5.1. In so doing, it clearly indicated that in order that a SPS measure could be set up 'on the basis' of an evaluation of the risks within the meaning of Article 5.1, it was necessary for there to be a 'logical' or 'objective' relationship between the measure and the evaluation of the risks. The Appeal Organ made it clear, moreover, that the risk to be evaluated, according to Article 5.1, is not only the risk that is verifiable under strictly controlled conditions in a scientific laboratory, but equally the risk in human societies such as exist in reality. Consequently, there were good grounds for taking into consideration in an evaluation of risks, according to Article 5.1, the risks resulting from the abusive use of hormones and the difficulty of controlling their use. See www.wto.org.

3   The Commission of the Codex Alimentarius was established by the conference of the FAO in 1961. Its aim is to develop international norms to facilitate trade in agricultural and alimentary products. In doing this, the FAO was pursuing the mandate given to it in 1943 to develop quality norms in order for international trade to meet the needs of the world's hungry population. In 1962, the integrated programme FAO/WTO was created and the Codex Alimentarius was the executive organ of it.

4   It is to be noted that the time taken by these organizations to develop norms is important. The three organizations, the CIPV, the Codex Alimentarius and the IOE have an obligation to report on the projects of norms to the different member countries and to the different committees of experts. The use of international norms facilitates the exchanges.

3 The Agreement on Technical Barriers to Trade

1   The agreement divides the technical regulations into two categories: those for which observance is obligatory and those for which this is only voluntary. A technical regulation is a document that sets out the characteristics of a product or the processes and methods of production (PMP) relating to it and observance of which obligatory. The standard is a document approved by a recognized body that provides, for common and repeated usage, rules, guidelines or characteristics for products or production processes for which observance is not compulsory.

2   According to Douglas Jake Caldwell, the object of packing is to communicate and inform the consumer by a description of the product's characteristics. Eco-packing communicates and informs the consumer about the environmental effect of the product. See www.itb.org.

3   India does have a programme but it is not applied.

4 The Agreement on Agriculture

1 Such as for the countries who are neither important exporters nor net importers and who must supply the alimentation needs of their population.

2 The lists are composed of public programmes financed by public funds (for example, services in research, inspection, training and commercialization, constitution of stocks for alimentary security, or public programmes of alimentary aid). The second category is composed of decoupled and direct subsidies to the producers (for example, support to income, aid in case of natural catastrophes, aid to disadvantaged regions, fight against aridity, protection of the environment).

3 Especially used in United States and in the member states of the EU.

4 The basic GSM is the sum of all internal support granted to agricultural producers during the 1986–1988 average base period, calculated by adding together all the global support measures for initial products, the global support measure other than by product, and all equivalent support measures for agricultural products (excluding exempted support and orange support whose total does not exceed the appropriate *de minimis* level).

5 This flexibility clause involves economic risks. When an economic production sector continues to receive subsidies for three consecutive years, it may be difficult to cut it off suddenly in the fourth year. This clause, moreover, cannot be the subject of a dispute settlement.

6 Poland called on this clause for sugar, and succeeded in exporting sugar to its main exporter, Thailand.

7 Document DG Agri (2000).

8 The Blue Box comprises US and EU direct payments to farmers who restrict their output or at least some inputs. These were granted exemption from challenge under the Blair House agreement to move the Uruguay Round talks forward.

5 The General Agreement on Trade in Services (GATS)

1 Commercial presence is composed of all the categories of business or establishment whose objective is to provide a service. They can offer this service in creating a new enterprise, in acquiring an enterprise or in establishing a branch.

2 For example, the services of a professional adviser can be provided in the framework of a visit by his or her foreign customer, by mail, by an office established in the customer country or by a personal visit to the customer country. On the contrary, a tourist cannot enjoy beaches unless he or she is visiting the country.

3 Defined as all agreements which cover all services and which translate into the phasing out of all discriminations.

4 The agreement does not specify whether the sectors concerned are sectors or subsectors. The agreement covers twelve sectors and 155 sub-sectors. Barriers to trade are also very different in the services, since national regulations that have an impact on the international trade in services are concerned – from which comes the importance of mutual recognition agreements. The problem is thornier for the DCs, which frequently have only a few regulations in the services area in comparison with the often sophisticated regulations of the developed countries.

5 As an example, the waste disposal service, which in France relies on a network for collecting the domestic waste, cannot use this network to ban a foreign company from settling in the country.

6 The Agreement on Intellectual Property Rights

1 The Paris Convention applies to invention patents, utility models, industrial designs, trademarks, service marks, corporate names and labels of origin, as well as the repression of unfair trading.
2 Copyrights concern all productions in the literary, scientific and artistic fields, irrespective of the mode or form of expression.
3 The Brazilian legislation stipulated that the manufacture of medicaments must be carried out on Brazilian territory. If this were not the case, the company would lose its patent at the end of three years. A compulsory patent was to be granted against the payment of royalties to the patent holder in the case of a national emergency.
4 Generics are locally manufactured products not covered by patents.
5 The latter are distinguishable from patents in that their novelty and inventiveness are not as advanced. They particularly apply to the mechanical domain.

7 Measures concerning trade-related investment

1 Section 301, introduced in 1974, authorized the US Trade Representative to take retaliatory measures in the case of unfair practices of a trading partner. This law applied to American imports as well as exports. The application of this law resulted in 25 petitions against the EU, 19 of which implicated the trade in services and 10 concerned international property rights. Almost half of the cases were settled by bilateral negotiations, and somewhat more than 12 cases gave rise to sanctions.
2 Investments are necessary for the provision of a service.

8 The Agreement on Textiles and Clothing

1 These figures, however, are unconfirmed. It is necessary to specify what 'world trade' covered. For example, all the trade between non-members of GATT (apart from China when it joined the MFA) excludes that between and with the countries from the East which was not covered by the MFA. Similarly, inter-community trade was not subject to the MFA, but is not counted in the world textile and clothing trade.
2 At first, the 1990 volume constituted the reference base, because it was important to know the integration that would be made by the biggest importers, the European Union and the USA. Certain countries had chosen value rather than volume, but 1990 was accepted as the base year because these statistics were the available statistics at the time of negotiation. If another year had been used as a reference point in the agreement, the parameters used as a base in the final negotiation would have to have been changed.
3 Covered by the provisions of Article 2 of the ATC.
4 In the case of wool products imported into the USA, the quota may be affected by a growth rate of 'not less than 2 per cent', document G/TMB/N/107.

9 The WTO and regional integration: compatible or contradictory?

1 Agreement between the Czech Republic and Slovakia on the occasion of the dissolution of Czechoslovakia.

2 The number of regional agreements is now between 150 to 200. Regional integration covers almost all the WTO members, except for Hong Kong, Japan and Korea. About 60 per cent of world trade is carried on outside MFN and is covered by preferential arrangements.

3 Article V is very recent. There are very few examples concerning this article. The rare examples are in the examination stage.

4 It is on this basis that the EU has frequently notified agreements concluded with third party countries after ratification. This was especially the case with the conclusion of the Euro-Mediterranean Agreements. During the conclusion of the European agreements, the EU did not notify the WTO, since the area of cooperation extended to the political domain, and the agreements had to be ratified by the national parliaments. But, at the same time, the EU concluded an interim agreement that only concerned trade clauses, and did notify this interim agreement to the WTO.

5 This expression 'global incidence' has been greatly debated. Following its adhesion to the EU, Sweden, which levied no duty on semi-conductors, started to impose a duty of about 10 to 15 per cent. Korea and Japan, which were big exporters to Sweden, lost their market. They then put forward the argument that globally these duties or regulations are possibly no higher or rigorous, but that in this specific area they are.

10 The Agreement on Rules of Origin

1 The SH is a decimal classification that applies to all merchandise. The first two figures define the chapter, the four first figures the position, and the six figures the sub-position. In the 1996 SH there is a total of 5,130 sub-positions.

2 The problem was exacerbated by the fact that some community products (mostly Italian rather than French) are considered by the American customs as originating from China or Pakistan, for example, with the result that this merchandise, despite being a community product for the exporters, can only be imported into the USA under a Chinese or Pakistani contingent (TVA). It concerns rather a problem of quotas than of taxes. The USA and the EU have arrived at an agreement suspending the application of the new rules of origin by the USA.

12 The WTO and developing countries: towards an equality of power

1 The Group of 10 consisted of five leaders – Argentina, Brazil, Egypt, India and Yugoslavia – joined by Chile, Jamaica, Pakistan, Peru and Uruguay as active members.

13 The emergence of new issues

1 The USA imposed an embargo on tuna fish coming from Mexico, because the nets used for the fishing were killing dolphins. The GATT had found this measure to be inconsistent with Article XX of the GATT, which applies to the product, or similar product, but not to the production process. According to Mexico, the Mexican tuna are similar products to those produced domestically, and the American regulation was attempting to attack the process of production of tuna that did not concern the characteristic of the product. The USA could not impose a method of fishing by virtue of its own legislation. In the second

tuna–dolphin case, the working party reconsidered this decision and ruled that the policy directed towards protecting the life and well-being of dolphins in the eastern tropical waters of the Pacific Ocean fell within the scope of Article XX of the GATT. The US Federal Appeal Court refused permission for the Trade Department to reduce the standards of labelling currently used in the sale of tuna. In the case of shrimps, the same reasoning had been invoked by the Dispute Settlement Body, which found that the measure taken by the USA in conditioning the access of shrimps to the American market according to the utilization of a certain method of fishing was inconsistent with Article XX. The USA could not unilaterally decide on a conservation policy for the species of another country.

2 The Secretariat recommended control by a tax of the consumption of substances that endanger the ozone layer, and the imposition of an embargo when coming from any country. These measures would be less restrictive for trade.

3 Australia introduced an embargo against fresh salmon from Canada. Canada made a complaint to the organ of dispute settlement.

4 This dispute came about between the USA and Japan. The USA requested consultation with Japan concerning the laws, regulations and requirements affecting the distribution and sale of imported photographic films and paper. The USA maintained that the Japanese government treated imported films less favourably than the domestic varieties, in violation of Articles III and X. The instruments of industrial policy applied by Japan deprived Kodak of access to its retail market. Since Fuji controlled the distribution networks, Kodak had to sell directly to the retailers, and this decreased its market penetration. The complaint therefore concerned the anti-competitive vertical relations between Fuji and the wholesalers. Japan contended that the wholesalers also bought imported films and that Kodak had its own distribution network, which had resulted in the creation of its own wholesale system. The working party concluded that the USA had not been able to demonstrate that the Japanese distribution measures had reduced Kodak's profits and that imported films were treated less favourably than those of domestic origin (Stephenson 2000: 133).

5 The geographical indications is a location which helps to identify a product, for example, Gruyère cheese or champagne.

Bibliography

All magazines and newspapers as quoted in the text.

Anderson, Kym, Erwidodo and Merlinda Ingco (1999) 'Integrating Agriculture into the WTO: The Next Phase', paper presented at the WTO/World Bank Conference on Developing Countries in a Millennium Round, WTO Secretariat, Geneva, 20–21 September.

Auboin, Marc and Laird, Sam (1997) *EU Import Measures and the Developing Countries*, Staff working papers TPRD 98–01.

Bergsten, Fred C. (1996) *Competitive Liberalization and Global Free Trade: A Vision for the Early 21st Century*, APEC Working Paper 96–15, Washington, DC: Institute for International Economics.

Bergsten, Fred C. (1998) *Fifty Years of the GATT/WTO: Lessons from the Past for Strategies for the Future*, Washington, DC: Institute for International Economics.

Burtless, Gary, Lawrence, Robert, Litan, Robert and Shapiro, Robert (1998) *Globophobia: Confronting Fears about Open Trade*, Washington, DC: The Brookings Institution.

Correa, Carlos (2000) *Intellectural Property Rights, the WTO and Developing Countries: The TRIPS Agreement and Policy Options*, London: Zed Books.

Cotter, Thomas (2001) *The WTO and Environmental Law: Some Issues and Ideas*, New York: Cambridge University Press.

Croome, John (1998) 'The Present Outlook for Trade Negotiations in the World Trade Organization' (http://www.wto.org).

D'Andrea Tyson, Laura (1992) *Who's Bashing Whom? Trade Conflict in High-Technology Industries*, Washington, DC: Institute for International Economics.

Das, Dilip (2000) 'Debacle at Seattle: The Way the Cookie Crumbled', *Journal of World Trade*, 34, 5.

Davey, William (2001) 'Has the WTO Dispute Settlement System Exceeded its Authority? A Consideration of Deference Shown by the System to Member Government Decisions and its Use of Issue-Avoidance Techniques', *Journal of International Economic Law*, 5.

De Joncquières, Guy (2000) 'Free Trade Under Fire: How Protectionists Are Winning the Battle for Public Opinion', in Roger Porter and Pierre Sauvé (eds) *Liberalizing Trade in Services*, Washington, DC: The Brookings Institution.

De Motta Veiga, Pedro, de Carvalho Jr, Mário C., Vilmar, Maria Lucia, Mucchielli, Façanha and Heraldiva (1997) 'Eco-Labelling Schemes in the European Union and the Impact on Brazilian Exports', in Simonetta Zarilli, Veena Jha and René Vossenaar (eds) *Eco-Labelling and International Trade*, London: Routledge, in association with UNCTAD, pp. 65–79.

Destler, I.M. (1995) *American Trade Policy*, third edition, Washington, DC: Institute for International Economics with the Twentieth Century Fund.

Elliott, Kimberly Ann (2000) 'M(is) Managing Diversity: Worker Rights and US Trade Policy', *International Negotiation*, 5(1).

Feketekuty, Geza (2000) 'Improving the Architecture of the General Agreement on Trade in Services', in Sherry Stephenson (ed.) *Services Trade in the Western Hemisphere: Liberalization, Integration and Reform*, Washington, DC: The Brookings Institution, pp. 19–42.

Finger, Michael and Messerlin, Patrick (1989) *The Effects of Industrial Countries' Policies on DCs*, Washington, DC: The World Bank.

Footer, Mary E. (2001) 'Developing Country Practice in the Matter of WTO Dispute Settlement', *Journal of World Trade*, 35(1).

Ganesan, A.V. (1998) *Strategic Options Available to DCs with Regard to a Multilateral Agreement on Investment*, Discussion Paper, no. 134, Geneva and New York: UNCTAD.

Ganesan, A.V. (2000) 'Seattle and Beyond', in Jeffrey J. Schott (ed.) *The WTO after Seattle*, Washington, DC: Institute for International Politics, pp. 85–87.

Goldstein, Judith (1993) 'Creating the GATT Rules: Politics, Institutions and American Policy', in John Ruggie (ed.) *Multilateralism Matters*, New York: Columbia University Press.

Gupta, Indrani and Nunnenkamp, Peter (1998) 'The Case of India', in Simonetta Zarilli and Colette Kinnon (eds) *International Trade in Health Service: A Development Perspective*, Geneva: United Nations and World Health Organization.

Habeeb, William Mark (1988) *Power and Tactics in International Negotiations: How Weak Nations Bargain with Strong Nations*, Baltimore, MD: The Johns Hopkins University Press.

Hart, Michael (1999) 'A Matter of Synergy: The Role of Regional Agreements in the Multilateral Trading System', in Donald Barry and Ronald Keith (eds) *Regionalism and Multilateralism and the Politics of Global Trade*, Vancouver: University of British Colombia Press.

Hoekman, Bernard (2000) 'Competition Policy and the Global Trading System: A Developing Country Perspective', http://www.worldbank.org

Homans, G. (1961) *Social Behavior: Its Elementary Forms*, New York: Harcourt, Brace and World.

Jackson John (2000) *The World Trading System: Law and Policy of International Economic Relations*, Cambridge, MA: The MIT University Press.

Jacquet, Pierre (2001) 'Comment', in Roger Porter, Pierre Sauvé Arvind Subramanian and Americo Beviglia Zampetti (eds) *The Multilateral Trading System at the Millennium, Efficiency, Equity, Legitimacy*, Washington, DC: The Brookings Institution.

Jander Harold and Inotai, Andràs (1996) 'Introduction', in Harold Jander and Andràs Inotai (eds) *The World Trade after the Uruguay Round: Prospects and Policy Options in the 21st Century*, London: Routledge.

Jönsson, Christer (1990) *Communication in International Bargaining*, London: Pinter Publishers.

Josling, Timothy and Tangermann, S. (1999) 'The Interests of Developing Countries in the Next Round of WTO Agricultural Negotiations', UNCTAD, paper presented to the workshop on Developing a Proactive and Coherent Trade Agenda, Pretoria, 29 June–2 July.

Kelman, Herbert C. (1996) 'Negotiation as Interactive Problem Solving', *International Negotiation*, 1(9).

Kennes, Walter (2000) *Small Developing Countries and Global Markets: Competing in the Big League*, New York: St Martin's Press.

Krueger, Anne (1999) 'The DCs and the Next Round of Multilateral Trade Negotiations', *Journal of World Trade*, 22(1).

Krueger, Anne *et al.* (1988) 'Agricultural Incentives in DCs: Measuring the Effects of Sectoral and Economy-wide Policies', *World Bank Economic Review*, 2(7).

Lal Das, Bhagirath (1999) 'Strengthening the Developing Countries in the WTO', in *International Monetary and Financial Issues for the 1990s*, New York: United Nations.

Landau, Alice (1996) *Conflits et coopérations dans les relations économiques internationales: Le cas de l'Uruguay round*, Bruxelles: Editions Emile Bruylant.

Landau, Alice (2000) 'Analyzing International Economic Negotiations: Towards a Synthesis of Approaches', *Journal of International Negotiation*, 5(1).

Landau, Alice (2001) *Redrawing the Global Economy: Elements of Integration and Fragmentation*, London: Macmillan.

Lawrence, Robert (2000) 'America's Interests in the Millennium Round', in Roger Porter and Pierre Sauvé (eds) *Seattle, the WTO and the Future of the Multilateral Trading System*, John F. Kennedy School of Government, Cambridge, MA: Harvard University Press.

Lowi, Philip and Baldock, David (2000) *The CAP Regime and the European Countryside: Prospects for Integration between Agricultural, Regional and Environmental Policies*, Allingford: CABI Publishers.

Markandya, Anil (1997) 'Eco-Labelling: An Introduction and Review', in Simonetta Zarilli, Veena Jha and René Vossenaar (eds) *Eco-Labelling and International Trade*, London: Routledge in association with UNCTAD.

Martin, Will and Winters, Alan (2000) *The WTO and DCs*, Cambridge: Cambridge University Press.

Maskus, Keith (2000) *Intellectual Property Rights in the Global Economy*, Washington, DC: Institute for International Economics.

Maskus, Keith (2000) *Regulatory Standards in the WTO: Comparing Intellectual Property Rights with Competition Policy, Environmental Protection, and Core Labor Standards*, Washington, DC: Institute for International Economics, Working Papers, http://www.iie.com

Matto, Aaditya (1999) 'Developing Countries in the New Round of GATS

Negotiations: From a Defensive to a Pro-active Role', paper presented at the WTO/World Bank Conference on Developing Countries in the Millennium Round, Geneva, 20–21 September.

Mavroidis, Petros (2000) 'Trade and Environment after the Shrimps–Turtles Litigation', *Journal of World Trade*, 34(1).

Mayasheki, Mina and Gibbs, Murray (1999) 'Lessons from the TRIMs Negotiations', *Journal of World Trade*, 26(1).

Messerlin, Patrick (1990) 'Antidumping', in Jeffrey J. Schott (ed.) *Completing the Uruguay Round*, Washington, DC: Institute for International Economics.

Michalopoulos, Constantine (1999) 'DCs. Strategies for the Millennium Round', *Journal of World Trade*, 33(5).

Michalopoulos, Constantine (2000) 'The Role of Special and Differential Treatment for DCs in GATT and the World Trade Organization', http://www.worldbank.org

Mukherjee, Neela (1999) 'GATS and the Millennium Round of Multilateral Negotiations, Selected Issues from the Perspective of the DCs', *Journal of World Trade*, 33(4).

Nicolaidis, Kalypso and Trachtman, Joel (2000) 'Liberalization, Regulation, and Recognition for Services Trade', in Sherry Stephenson (ed.) *Services Trade in the Western Hemisphere: Liberalization, Integration and Reform*, Washington, DC: The Brookings Institution Press, pp. 43–71.

Organization of African Unity (1994) *Report of the Secretary General on Preliminary Evaluation Results of the Uruguay Round of Multilateral Trade Negotiations of the General Agreement on Tariffs and Trade (GATT)*, Addis Ababa: OAU.

Ostry, Sylvia (2000) 'Convergence and Sovereignty' in Aseem Prakash and Jeffrey Hart (eds) *Coping with Globalization*, London: Routledge, pp. 52–76.

Pardo Quintillãn, Sara (1999) 'Free Trade, Public Health Protection and Consumer Information in the European and WTO Context: Hormone-Treated Beef and Genetically Modified Organisms', *Journal of World Trade* (33)6.

Park, Young Duk and Umbricht, George (2001) 'WTOP Dispute Settlement, 1995–2000: A Statistical Analysis', *Journal of International Law*, 4(1): 16.

Perdikis, Nicholas, Kerr, William and Hobbs, Jill (2001) 'Reforming the WTO to Defuse Potential Trade Conflicts in Genetically Modified Goods', *The World Economy*, 24(3).

Pinell, James (2001) 'Agreement on Textiles and Clothing, Presenter's Brief', ITC.

Prakash, Aseem and Hart, Jeffrey (2000) 'Coping with Globalization: An Introduction' in Aseem Prakash and Jeffrey Hart (eds) *Coping with Globalization*, London: Routledge, pp. 1–26.

Prieto, Francisco Javier and Stephenson, Sherry (1999) 'Multilateral and Regional Liberalization of Trade in Services', paper presented at the World Services Congress, Atlanta, 1–3 November.

Primo Braga, Carlos (1996) 'Trade Related Intellectual Property Issues: The Uruguay Round Agreement and Its Economic Implications', in Will Marin and Alan Winters (eds) *The Uruguay Round and the Developing Countries*, Cambridge: Cambridge University Press, pp. 344–369.

Qureshi, Asif (1996) *The World Trade Organisation: Implementing International Trade Standards*, Manchester: Manchester University Press.

Raghavan, Chakravarthi (1996) *The 'New Issues' and DCs: Environment, Competition and Labour Standards*, Background Paper, Seminar of the WTO and DCs, Geneva, 10–11 September, p. 11.

Rhodes, Carolyn (1999) 'The European Union and the United States: A New Balance of Influence in the Global Political Economy', in Donald Barry and Ronald Keith (eds) *Regionalism, Multilateralism, and the Politics of Global Trade*, Vancouver: UBC Press.

Ricupero, Rubens (1998) 'Integration of DCs into the Multilateral Trading System', in Jadish Bagwati and Mattias Hirsch (eds) *The Uruguay Round and Beyond: Essays in Honor of Arthur Dunkel*, Ann Arbor, MI: University of Michigan Press, pp. 11–36.

Rodrik, Dani (1995) 'DCs after the Uruguay Round', in *International Monetary and Financial Issues for the 1990s*, Geneva: United Nations.

Ruigrok, W. and van Tulder, R. (1995) *The Logic of International Restructuring*, London: Routledge.

Runge, C. Ford, and Jackson, Lee Ann (2000) 'Labelling, Trade and Genetically Modified Organisms: A Proposed Solution', *Journal of World Trade*, 34(1).

Rutgers, Ann (1999) 'Trade and Environment: Reconciling the Montreal Protocol and the GATT', *Journal of World Trade*, 33(4).

Shafaedin, Mehdi (2000) *What Did Frederick List Actually Say? Some Clarifications on the Infant Industry Argument*, Discussion Paper No. 149. Geneva: United Nations.

Shahin, Magda (1997) 'Multilateral Investment and Competition Rules in the World Trade Organization: An Assessment', *Transnational Corporations*, 6(2).

Skogstad, Grace (1998) 'Ideas, Paradigms and Institutions: Agricultural Exceptionalism in the European Union and the United States', *Governance*, 4(11).

Smith, Pamela (1995) 'International Patent Protection and United States Exports: Evidence in the Data', paper presented at the conference, 'International Relations of Intellectual Property: Challenges at the Turn of the Century', Washington, DC: The American University.

Snape, Richard (1998) 'Reaching Effective Agreement Covering Services', in Ann Krueger (ed.) *WTO as an International Organisation*, Chicago: University of Chicago Press, pp. 279–292.

Srinavasan, T.N. (1999) 'DCs in the World Trading System: From GATT, 1947, to the Third Ministerial Meeting of the WTO, 1999', *Journal of World Trade*, 22(1).

Steinberg Richard and Stokes, Bruce (eds) (1998) *Partners or Competitors? The Prospects for US–European Cooperation on Asian Trade*, London: Rowman & Littlefield.

Stephenson, Sherry M. (2000) *Services Trade in the Western Hemisphere: Liberalization, Integration, and Reform*, Washington, DC: The Brookings Institution.

Stevens, Christopher (1996) 'Consequences of the Uruguay Round on DCs', in

Harold Jander and Andràs Inotai (eds) *The World Trade after the Uruguay Round: Prospects and Policy Options in the 21st Century*, London: Routledge, pp. 71–88.

UNCTAD (1994a) *The Outcome of the Uruguay Round: An Initial Assessment, Supporting Papers to the Trade and Development Report*, New York: United Nations.

UNCTAD (1994b) *Review of the Implementation, Maintenance, Improvement and Utilization of the Generalized System of Preference*, New York: United Nations.

UNCTAD (1999) *Report on Trade and Development*, Geneva: United Nations.

US General Accounting Office (1993) *The North American Free Trade Agreement*, Washington, DC.

Warkentin, Craig and Mingst, Karen (2000) 'International Institutions, the State and Global Civil Society in the Age of the World Wide Web', *Global Governance*, 20(3).

Wattal, Jayashree (2000) 'Developing Countries' Interests in a "Development Round"' in Jeffrey J. Schott (ed.) *The WTO after Seattle*, Washington, DC: Institute for International Economics.

Wilkinson, Rorden and Hughes, Steve (2000) 'Labor Standards and Global Governance: Examining the Dimensions of Institutional Engagement', *Global Governance*, 6(1).

The World Bank (1997) *World Development Report: The State in a Changing World*, Washington, DC: The World Bank.

WTO Secretariat (1999) document S/C/W/95, 9 February, p. 11.

WTO Secretariat (2001) Note, 10 July, MTN.GNS/W/120.

Zartman, William (1986) 'Importance of North–South Negotiations', in William Zartman (ed.) *Positive Sum: Improving North–South Negotiations*, New Brunswick, NJ: Transaction Books, pp. 278–301.

Index